DREW

BARRYMORE

BIOGRAPHY

Portrait of a life of women with wildflowers

Tasha Christine Kennedy

CONTENTS

CHAPTER 1

DOUBLE BOGEY

CHAPTER 2

LOCO MOTION

CHAPTER 3

UNSAFE AT ANY SPEED

CHAPTER 4

EXILE ON PAIN STREET

CHAPTER 5

WHAT TO EXPECT FROM MY BACK IN THE FUTURE

CHAPTER 6

SHOWING SOME SPINE

INTRODUCTION

CHAPTER 1

PARADISE BIRDS

West Hollywood, the neighbourhood where I grew up, was a vibrant place in 1975. Ildiko Jaid, my mother at the time, raised me as a single mother there. She was an ambitious actress who held two jobs, one at the prominent Comedy Store and the other at the infamous music club the Troubadour. She was surrounded by many wild artists, and the entire milieu at the time was highly hedonistic. She was also friends with a lot of gay men, so it just became a part of her life.

Joanie Goodfellow was our next-door neighbour on the other side of the duplex. Her son's name was Daniel Faircloth, and it wasn't until years later that I realised how different their names were. At the time, she was just another single mother, like mine, whose boyfriend had abandoned her and her child. Her son, Daniel, became my best friend, despite the fact that I had no idea what that meant at the time. But we'd go up and down the street selling apples and beating each other up. I believe this is a typical West Hollywood friendship. Each of our duplexes featured two bedrooms. It appeared to be quite large to me. I was truly proud that these single mothers could offer us a two-bedroom apartment. It was nothing to scoff at to have our own quarters. In addition, there was a teeny-tiny backyard with a cheap swing set and an avocado tree. It's hardly an exaggeration to say I ate ten avocados a day from that tree. That tree was fantastic. It sustained me, and it was my only source of nature, except from the flowing bougainvillaea out front.

Joanie and Daniel left when I was about four or five years old. I was depressed. But then this really sweet couple moved in with their Dalmatian named McBarker. Gina and Joel were a cute, handsome, and lovely couple, and I was immediately drawn to them. Especially Joel, as I was looking for someone "straightforward," like an uncomplicated male! There was no question of "are you gay, straight, a man or a woman?"—I realise you're not my father, but won't you be my neighbour, as Mr. Rogers would say? They were fantastic. On their side of the duplex, we all enjoyed Christmas together.

These were the most secure and pleasant years of my life. We resided in this house for seven years, as far back as I can remember. But when I was seven, when E.T. had opened and I was getting a number of other film offers, my mother's and my lives began to change. I'll never forget the night my mum arrived at the duplex with a brand-new BMW 320i while we were all waiting to go to supper together. I couldn't figure it out. Where had the battered Karmann Ghia gone? What was going on? Change was unsettling. We all went out to lunch, and I had the feeling I was on a horrible trip. It didn't sit well with me. A few weeks later, I returned home and stared up in terror as I approached the duplex. The bougainvillaea shrub had been felled. I began to cry. This was our entire house's cover. It was stunning. It was all natural. It was the thing that made me say, we don't have much money, but you don't need money to be amazed! This massive crimson waterfall has vanished. Terrified, I hurried back to the avocado tree. It was still there, but it had been shaved totally. That's when I first heard the term "pruned." My stomach dropped. It was only a trunk and a few branches. I was assured that it will grow back and that this was necessary in order for it to be healthy. I was ill. We'd been here for seven years and no one had clipped or manicured anything! Was a new gardener hired? What about the car? I was running in circles. Everything seemed to be collapsing around me.

Then it occurred to me: What condition were the birds of paradise in? I walked over to the side of the house where Joel had parked his ancient Mustang. Were those bizarre birds of paradise unharmed, or did they too receive royal treatment? I walked around the corner, one foot in front of the other, anticipating the surprise... and then I saw them. No heads on green stalks. They had not escaped whatever came here and snatched everything away from them. They were no longer threatening. They'd been guillotined and were now waiting for rebirth. And I felt heartbreak for the first time. They deserved nothing. They were certainly distinct. Sure, I'd never fully grasped them. But just now, all I wanted to do was hold them and tell them everything was fine. Then I realised I wasn't sure if it would. None of this made sense to me.

Later, my mother returned home; she had quit her work and informed me that she would be managing my career full-time. Then she dropped the bombshell: "We're moving to the valley!" I bought a house, and we'll have a genuine home!"—as if it were a selling factor. I was appalled. Great. I will be the primary breadwinner. We'll leave Joel, Gina, and McBarker behind and travel to what felt like another planet. We collected our belongings and moved into our new home, in Sherman Oaks, in 1983, as if I had been lobotomized. It's the reason I still speak like a valley girl.

I was resolved to return to headquarters as an adult, so I relocated to West Hollywood. I was now in authority of my own fate, and I bought a house in the old neighbourhood. I wanted to be in my comfort zone.

CHAPTER 2

FLYING HIGH

We'd heard about a skydiving facility not far from our house. Cameron Diaz and I were in a crazy phase where all we wanted to do was try new things. We'd become total adrenaline junkies after the buzz of Charlie's Angels and four months of kung fu training followed by six months of stunts. We'd just returned from the Tahitian Islands, where we'd scuba dived with sharks! It was incredible. We continued our trip as friends and thrill seekers long after the films stopped.

I've known Poo Poo (our mutual nickname for each other) since I was fourteen and she was sixteen. We first met in West Hollywood in the late 1980s. Cameron and Cory, two stunning models, were present. Everyone stared, but the most important thing was that they were both really lovely and the polar opposite of frigid. They were, however, cool.

So here we were, two females who wanted to jump out of an aircraft, viewing our training movies, which were terrible, but much worse, they required you to sign your life away. Literally. You must sign a "if I don't make it" agreement. They claim it's a routine procedure. They also warn you that you will most likely acquire cotton mouth on the flight up and to pack some water. What in the world was I doing? They handed us our suits to change into just as I was beginning to wonder if we had gone too far this time. Hers was bright crimson, while mine was canary yellow. We entered the changing rooms with our balled-up stuff. As we changed, the men were cracking jokes and yukking it up. I was getting the impression that these jerks were holding back from going head over heels for her. They were obviously salivating, and who wouldn't be?

I'm delighted to report that I arrived safely after what seemed like an eternity. My instructor kissed me on the cheek like a grandmother. Yuck. Thank you very much. You put me in this clown costume, and now you want to grope me? I need to get out of here. We got out of there as quickly as we could, grateful to have our lives and bodies intact. And then we drove to the nearest watering hole we could find. We dashed inside a fast-food restaurant on the side of the road. We repeated our experiences in words after two sodas and two burritos— A, since we could finally chat without being interrupted, and B, because my mouth was working again.

Poo Poo bit through glass in her burrito just as we were getting started and silently wailing over what we were each going through. If it's not one thing, it's something else. You survive falling out of a plane, but you nearly die after eating. We just burst out laughing, the loudest you could imagine. We took off and drove back to Hollywood with the wind in our faces through the open windows of the car—though I think it's safe to say that wind in my face like that of a free fall at ten thousand feet will never happen again.

We're both older now, and she's still one of my best pals. I was her bridesmaid, and she is the godmother of my daughter Frankie. We still go on adventures, but they are considerably more relaxed. But that's what I like about my pal. She's always up for a game. And I'll always be her young man.

CHAPTER 3

MY BEAUTIFUL LAUNDRETTE

The courts granted me emancipation when I was fourteen. It's no secret that I had to split up with my mother since we had destroyed our relationship. She had ruined her reputation as a mother by taking me to Studio 54 (wrong but enjoyable) instead of school.

My mother was there at my hearing and fully supported my emancipation, which would mean living on my own. I was heartbroken, yet so much had transpired. The judge entered, and the rest of the day flew by. People testified, yet the atmosphere was neither gloomy or sombre. It was a way of asking, "Should this kid grow up?" The judge looked at me at the conclusion of the day and said something that resonated with me: "I can turn the clock forward, but I can never turn it back." "Are you prepared for that?" "Yes," I said. "OK," he continued, smiling slightly, "I hereby proclaim you an adult!" Legally." My mother and I hugged, knowing that things would be different, but things were always too different, which is why this had to happen.

From the perspective of the state of California, I walked out as an eighteen-year-old. This was going to be a lot of fun.

The first item on my checklist was...

1. Residence!

I scoured West Hollywood, my favourite neighbourhood and where I grew up. I located a room in the back of a building where my buddy Justine lived. Great! Despite the fact that it was off an alleyway in a notoriously "don't walk around here at night" neighbourhood, I was relieved that my fiancée was only a short distance away. She lived there with her boyfriend, and I enjoyed it when they fought. I was always secretly hoping they would divorce since I fantasised about Justine and me having our own bungalow somewhere!

2. Job.

Justine worked at a coffee shop in the valley, but she had a car, and I was still two years away from acquiring my driver's licence, so I'd have to act globally while thinking locally. Inspired by Justine, I went to a nearby coffee shop, the Living Room, which happened to be a popular nighttime hangout in Los Angeles. It was the early 1990s, when everyone hung out in coffeehouses. Every night, people spilled out onto the street, as if it were a great art opening, although it was just an ordinary Tuesday.

I wasn't very good at my job. I wasn't particularly talented in any area. I'd only done two things: acted and lived in the wilderness. However, neither of these prepares you for life in the real world.

The next day, I went to work, and I could see my supervisor, who had hired me on the unique notion of having a washed-up former child actor behind the counter, was tolerant with all of my learning curves but also irritated with me. "You have to be present for the muffin deliveries!" At precisely seven a.m.! Otherwise, we'll run out of things to put in the damn cases!!!" "OK, you got it." It was a bit in one ear and out the other. Another time, he came in while I was doing dishes (which, come to think of it, probably subconsciously made me realise you had to "do" dishes rather than just throw everything in the sink and pray, as I used to do at home), but he walked in and said, very sharply and exasperatedly, "Don't use the abrasive side of the brush!!!!" All of the pastry casings are becoming scratched and hazy, making it impossible to see what's within!!!!" "Oh, you're correct! I thought it was cleaning it up, but I see what you mean! "Hmm, I'm not sure why that was happening." He glanced at me with wide eyes and then moved into another room, definitely muttering "idiot" under his breath. But, once again, he liked me, and I had genuinely wrecked certain things. He had every reason to be irritated.

I returned to my flat after work, feeling like a loser. I had a peek around the filthy apartment. Everything I touched became garbage. The refrigerator! The drain! The furniture, which was in fifty pieces, lay motionless on the floor. And don't forget about the laundry! I had no idea what I was wearing because everything I owned was in that basket, mocking me... AAAAAAAARRRRRRGGGGGGGGGGGGGGGG. I threw myself onto the bed, clutching my pillow and stared at the wall all night. I knew I'd made it through another night when the sun crept into the eerie alley outside my bedroom window. But this was not what I had in mind when I walked out of the courthouse with a spring in my step. Somehow, something had to give. I adored self-improvement movie montages and had to make my own! Start the music! So, what did I require?

First, the fundamentals!

Toilet tissue.

Sponge.

Soap.

Vacuum. (Intimidating!)

Somebody assembled my furniture.

The bedside table.

Lamp.

More books for that table, please.

Yeah, books, books, books! Books make me happy and make me feel less alone.

I chipped away at things one by one. But where the montage really started to soar was when I walked into a store to buy a laundry basket. There were all sorts of shapes and sizes, a whole wall of baskets. After holding different ones—as I knew I would be hoofing it several blocks to a Laundromat and I needed it to fit my body—I picked one and walked out with my brand-new vessel.

I bought detergent, bleach, and fabric softener. I grabbed my book and enough clothes to fill the basket sensibly and headed out the door. In my maiden voyage to the Laundromat, the whole way I was talking to myself . . . Bleach first, detergent, wait, first cycle has bleach and detergent? That doesn't sound right. And the liquid fabric softener goes in the dryer? But isn't that going to make the clothes wet all over again? I was very confused. It doesn't seem like all three go into the wash? What? No! I had given myself a stomach ache. I walked in. I went to the machines. Which ones were which? Was this the washer or the dryer? What the hell? The circle shapes all around started to close in on me. I was Michael Keaton in Mr. Mom before he figured it all out! I was screwed. I just stood there. After a while, like a kid cheating on a test, I just started to spy on whatever other people were doing. OK, that guy is pulling out wet clothes, so that must be the WASHER. Aha! Got it! Right. It was also the kind of place where some of the washers were upright so the washer and the dryer looked the same, stacked on top of each other, which confused me so much because I was convinced all the water would come pouring out and I would make the biggest fool out of myself ever.

Eventually I put some clothes in the washer, but then, did I put the liquid right in the clothes??? Wait, is this going to stain everything??? Oh God! And the bleach smells like it's going to disintegrate my clothes on the spot!!! Needless to say I put the bleach directly on the clothes and then I put the liquid fabric softener right in the dryer.

When I pulled out the Dalmatian-spotted jeans and the gummy towels, I knew I had done it all wrong, but there was always a next time and the next time would include Justine! I clearly needed a tutorial.

She came with me and gave me some tips and direction! It was a revelation! Of course! It all made such sense! Wow! The whole movie went from '80s comedy to glorious black-and-white! Yes, the opposite! But that's what I wanted in this new world I was creating for myself. It was the romance I was waiting for. Think of an old French movie!

Every weekend I would look forward to this ritual. I didn't feel alone there. I could be domestic, read my book, and eat some Chinese from the place next door in a carton with chopsticks. Everything fell into place, and I got so good at laundry that it became a point of pride. I loved stain removal. The art of getting your whites white. Pouring in my fabric softener and bleach so that I was more of a chef making a stew getting the ratios and flavours just right! And once I had finished my classic novel, I was excited to go to the bookstore and get a new one. I read books by Tolstoy, Jane Austen, Joan Didion, Bukowski, John Fante, and Kurt Vonnegut. The Fountainhead. To

Kill a Mockingbird. I read everything. What was my next adventure going to be? As I roamed the book aisles, I had a realisation that I had dropped out of school. Once I was emancipated, I just simply dropped out. Oh my God!!! I had a pit in my stomach again. What was I going to do? I had been on film sets my whole life, receiving three hours a day of tutoring. I hated when I went back to school because kids were merciless, a chapter you are supposed to face, but fuck it, I had enough to face at this point, I wasn't going back voluntarily, but what??? I didn't want to be uneducated. Oh my God, oh my God???? Just when I had mastered laundry, I was panicking all over again. What did I want to learn?

What was my vocation? Tears. I'm not sure. I used to perform, but that's all over now, and I'm not sure if they'll hire me again. People believed I was insane, even though I wasn't; I simply grew up too quickly! Aaaarrrrgggghhhh. OK, get your act together. The book walls began to engulf me. When I looked at all the bindings, jackets, shelves, titles, and fonts, I began to feel more grounded. The book jackets relaxed me, and I continue to appreciate this practice to this day. Books? Book wisely? I am able to read. I adore literature. Everyone seems to take pride in being well-read. Books not only make me happy, but they are also excellent for me! Healthy. Screw that! I'm going to start my own school! I can self-educate if I can live on my own! I'm going to get a dictionary and go through every word. I'm going to immerse myself in whatever I enjoy! I adore doing laundry! I adore books! I adore music! I guess I appreciate art (go to museums immediately!). I made the decision right then and there that I would not be defeated. Failure was out of the question! I'd design my own curriculum.

That's exactly what I did! I read! I did the cleaning! I was employed! Oh my goodness, work! My supervisor was having another "you suck at this" moment with me back at the coffee shop. And as I was describing another thing I'd botched up, he stared at me with those saucer eyes one last time and whispered, clenched teeth, "Why don't you go out and find yourself!" And, despite the fact that he was partially trying to get rid of me, he was half right! This wasn't it, I realised as I looked about. This was not my fate. That was the day I stopped. I returned to my apartment and went right up to Justine's door, knocking fervently (word of the day from my annotated dictionary) until she opened it. "Would you ever want to move out and be roommates if I found us a new place to live and get the hell out of this shithole?" She gave me a look. "Well, Darren and I just divorced, so sure!" I'm in." Yaaaaaaaaaaay! I have a roommate!!! This could potentially be entertaining! I dashed back to my flat and began circling apartments for rent in the newspaper. I peered out my window, listening to the cats fighting in the alley, and waited for the sun to come up to tell me everything was well. That it was. I wasn't afraid any longer. I was prepared! Even though it was merely washing, it taught me how to deal with anything in the future. You fall in love and want to conquer it by mastering it!

CHAPTER 4

TAURUS

When Nan and I founded our firm, Flower Films, we began to actually explain our idea. We wanted to share our experiences. We resolved not to give up our JanSport backpacks during the power-suit woman era of the early 1990s. But all we'd do was schoolwork all the time. We researched everything. We prepared checklists for everything. Everything is read by us. And instead of partying with the gorgeous people, we formed relationships with people we admired and respected.

At Flower Films on Sunset Boulevard, we created a homey atmosphere. Nan's office was comfortable and lived in. All of our chats and dreams took place there. Her workplace was welcoming and well-organised, with everything labelled. Inbox, outbox, photographs on the wall, pillows, and Abraham Lincoln mantras in small frames on her desk. My office was a disorganised mess, with papers all over the place and no feng shui at all. We exchanged

Christmas cards every year, and it felt like we were starting traditions that I had never had. Outside of work, we would travel across America in an RV. We planned to travel throughout the world. We'd get some dogs. The most essential thing to remember about Nan is that she never let me get away with anything.

We always emerge stronger from our experiences. I spent most of my childhood holidays with her family; she was the maid of honour at my wedding; and she is the family I never had until I created my own. And she is still. She has been my light and kindness for the past 22 years. She's also the most entertaining person I've ever met. And if you want the best love advice, look no further. We've created numerous films about relationships, including Fever Pitch, in which she met her husband, Jimmy Fallon, and the beautiful lady met the perfect guy. And, as much as she despises the term "perfect," she is to me.

She would also advise me that writing was the finest thing to do when I was feeling lost! And as a journal enthusiast, this really spoke to me. After Olive was born, another person I adore, Kate Capshaw Spielberg (Scorpio!), surprised me with a five-year notebook. And when I was a brand-new mother facing unprecedented dread and stress, this pink leather-bound diary was delivered to my door with a letter that stated, "Start writing to your daughter and keep it up every day!" Kate, love." I held this notebook care box in my hand and remembered what Nan always said. And I've written in it every day since then, charting Frankie and Olive's lives, and it will be my gift to them when they're older.

So, who exactly was I in this hospital room? Was I a damaged child with mother issues, or was I a lady who went out there and fought hard for her lessons, finding amazing role models? Great people, such as Nan, have led me and lifted me out of a state of helplessness or fear, and have given me power. Now I must pass on my knowledge and strength. Was I going to hide in here when this youngster, this new and gorgeous infant, needed me? No way, no how. Sore and groggy, I got up and grabbed up my baby Taurus. And I kissed her face repeatedly. I vowed, just like Olive, that I would always be her protector. Their Pisces mother is me. Dragoness, Mother of Dragons! I am powerful. I've discovered something new. I adore Love and have plenty to offer. My tremendous destiny requires me to grow two decent girls into two wonderful women! Okay, fine. Here we go, my lovely little girls. Let's get started.

CHAPTER 5

BRONCO

My car had no name; it was merely a metaphor for my life. "Wild." "Bull in the china shop." "Reckless." I was about seventeen years old and still lived in West Hollywood. Going on auditions again in order to resurrect my career, but not in the spotlight. I was alone with my Bronco.

The incredible thing about the late 1980s and early 1990s was that there was no Internet. There were no digital cameras. If you wanted to share a photograph, you would have to first develop it and then deliver it in person. And no one gave a damn. It was the one time in my life when everyone was in their own bubble, when widespread voyeurism had not yet emerged, and when sharing simply did not exist.

I'd drive around LA in my big Bronco, just enjoying the wind in my hair. I have no recollection of what I did that day. Some days, staying in the cabin while going through the vehicle wash and watching the soap and bubbles fall down the windshield would be the highlight. Everything was a haze. Everything would come alive at night, as if I were just waiting for the sky to change colour and the days didn't really matter. I slept late, wasn't expected anywhere, and didn't have anything to do. My responsibilities included making sure the automobile had enough gas and a nice mixtape in the car sound. So we'd drive around the hills, pulling pranks on people. "Pull over, pull over," Mel would say over the megaphone. This is the deer patrol, and your driving is endangering them. "Pull over," the terrified motorist would say, and we'd drive by laughing.

We were at a music event on the Sunset Strip one night on New Year's Eve—some hipster band, though that phrase was not yet widely used—and it was a fantastic riot, and I left feeling invincible, as one does after a good rock show. When I went to grab my Bronco from the parking lot down the street, I discovered it was closed. And I don't mean closed. A twenty-foot-tall gate with no signs of life. We had more exciting parties to attend, and I was not going to take this lying down.

Justine and Mel starred as I defied gravity by climbing the gate and leaping over it. I found my car, opened it, climbed into the driver's seat, and slammed it into reverse. As a result, I drove carefully up to the gate. Justine and Mel were standing on the other side, waiting, with the headlights in their eyes. I had a feeling we could get out of here. That massive fence was not going to stop me from getting into my car and completing our evening. I stood there staring at the gate, engine revving. I considered how I would go about doing this. I deduced that the first step would be to go as far back as I could before shifting into drive. In my mind's eye, I'd slam the gate with one fast slam, like ripping off a Band-Aid, and the force would just pop it open. It would be swift and accurate, and that would be the end of it. Bam. Literally.

That is exactly what I did. I rolled back slowly, a gleam in my eye, as I stared out the windshield at my target. I took hold of the steering wheel shifter and shifted into drive. I took a deep breath and pressed the gas pedal. I knew I'd have to hit the brakes hard because once I broke past the gate, I'd be on Sunset Boulevard in the blink of an eye. As a result, I drove with two feet. As I sped into the parking lot, I began to wonder if I should simply slam on the brakes and call it quits. "No way," I said, and drove through the gate. Justine and Mel scrunched their mouths, as if they were eating a lemon, while they awaited the blow. My Bronco slammed into the gate with a horrible metal-tearing bang, and instead of popping it up like a button, my hood forced the bottom of the gate up and it suddenly went flat like it was lying down.

Now that the gate was horizontal rather than vertical, I rapidly considered my next move. A crowd gathered to see what was making those strange sounds. To get out from under it, I swiftly shifted into reverse. I was back where I had started.

I should have given up at this point, but something took control and I felt this gate was no match for my Bronco and myself. I lost my senses and went for a second run. When I rammed the gate again, the modest crowd cheered like kids at a '80s movie party. The part where someone does something insane but everyone cheers them on. However, there was no activity at the gate. It was inclined 10 degrees higher up, as though someone was resting in traction.

I did it again. The audience began to grow in size. On New Year's Eve, Sunset Boulevard was crawling with inebriated revellers. You couldn't ask for a bigger crowd to cheer on a crazy girl driving her Bronco through a gate to get to the next party. Another smash! The gate appeared to be tumbling backwards this time. Of course, I couldn't see how my car seemed in front of me. I suddenly noticed the boxing ring's gate was ready to close. With one more massive punch, this creature lay on the ground, with no intention of restarting the fight. I was irrational and completely devoid of decent judgement, if any judgement at all.

The crowd was chanting by this point. My pals only stared at me, as though they knew I had it in me, but this was too far. They weren't as insane as I was. I turned around and took one last deep breath. I started the automobile by depressing the gas pedal while keeping my foot on the brake, so that when I let go, I would be travelling at full speed. I dashed forward, finally removing this motherfucking barrier.

It officially went up over my hood and laid on the ground in my rearview mirror, lifeless and mangled. The audience erupted. Looking out the window, I saw people high-fiving and cheering. In the rearview mirror: a lifeless gate. Windshield: celebration. It was an unusual polarity. The applause soon faded down, and people dispersed, returning to their own New Year's Eve world. However, no one recorded it. It was never mentioned to me. It was simply a wild moment that became a crazy moment. My companions and I got in the car and drove away. I didn't know what to think. The only emotion I felt was pride for my car. I knew we couldn't be stopped.

In the light of day the next morning, I examined my beloved Bronco. I wasn't a morning person to begin with, but this day was especially bright, and God was revealing what I had done. The devastation was severe. The entire front of the car appeared to have gone through a paper shredder. I felt dumb and humiliated. Is this who I used to be? Here comes the child-star footnote. Yikes. I drove the automobile into the dealership with my head down and my tail between my legs. I didn't have any parents to embarrass me, so I did it to myself. That, in fact, was the crux of the issue. I was still a child with no adult supervision. I had only me. That's why I always feel so bad when I'm incorrect. Because I am the only one who has noticed it and made an argument for being better. I was at odds with myself because I knew a part of me wanted to ram cars and feel invincible. But I knew there was a part of me that realised there was, at best, a time and place for it. As an actor, I could see myself in any situation or as any person. And at this point, I was completely convinced that I needed a more effective channel than just me and my Bronco. On a scorching day in the San Fernando Valley, I sat at the showroom, thinking, I need a new automobile, and I need a new life.

CHAPTER 6

THE BLUE ANGEL

The Blue Angel was a nightclub in New York. regularly was located deep within the Lower East Side, and my friends and I frequented regularly. It was a run-down performance space with one small stage and dim lighting. I donned the moniker Lolita and took my place on the stage. As the scene progressed, I was inspired to twirl around like a slow-motion 1960s-movie go-go dancer and strip off my clothes behind him, piece by piece. As this was a performance art venue, I seemed to do just that. We both decided it was time to wrap it up and let the curtain fall when I was like a little wood nymph behind him. It was over in the blink of an eye, and our wild little show was over before it had really begun.

In my life, I was incredibly liberated. As a mother, I struggle with this because, now that I am an adult, I am more concerned than ever about being suitable. I had to figure out for myself what was appropriate or not. I ran naked through fields and on beaches. During my great period of self-discovery, I was even featured in periodicals. I was on the cover of Rolling Stone wearing nothing but a flower-filled bathtub. I was working with some of the most talented and well-known photographers. I mistook myself for an artist. And I was completely in exhibitionist mode, not realising there was a term for it.

The night of the broadcast was David Letterman's birthday, thus the atmosphere was joyful. I was onstage when we began discussing the incident downtown. He and I were teasing each other. Having a nice time and laughing. I felt secure. While I was telling it, I had the unexpected inspiration to start acting it out. I was up on his desk before I could even think. Trust me, if I had thought it through, it would not have turned out that way. That was just another instance of utterly unplanned silliness that took off like a runaway train. It would have felt that way if I was attempting to be seductive or attract attention. You could see me trying to catch up to the moving train, and once I was dancing on his desk, I believe I was thinking about how I could up the ante and strike a finishing moment, and bam! I quickly lifted my top, only for David, where no one else could see.

I was startled at myself, and again, feeling as if the train was ahead of me, I whirled around, flung my arms up in the air, and stared at the audience, as if I had just done something stupid. Is this acceptable? Is there something wrong with me? I was completely unaware. But then I realised it was time to leave the desk and return to my chair, and on my way there, I grabbed David by the tie and pulled him in for a beautiful kiss on the cheek. And that was sweet, but what he thought of the entire situation hung in the balance. Thank God, he laughed and threw his head back. He made it clear to everyone that it was fine to enjoy the moment and not overthink it. This was a truly liberating experience. And it has to be something enjoyable rather than something negative. Dave, I appreciate it.

When we got in the car, I understood this might cause a stir. I hooked up with my Lower East Side buddies and we watched the show together when it aired that night. As the performance began, I commented, "Um, so this might be a little crazy," and they asked why, to which I replied, "Let's just watch," which we did. My pals were astonished but elated when my dance on the desk began to fly, and the whole thing finished in shouts with people shouting "Oh my God" and "I can't believe it." They weren't condemning me, but they weren't encouraging it either. Wow. I'd done something incredibly daring by putting it all out there. As I stood there objectively watching myself and my friends laugh, I understood that this was the end of an era for me.

So I began my journey into no sex scenes in movies, modesty restrictions in my contracts, and a complete lack of nudity in every public arena from that point forward. Year after year, I became more tense. One button up on the blouse and one inch down on the skirt.

Even though it went so well and couldn't have ended on a more fun note, I decided to take matters into my own hands. I knew that film had been my big break in the past, and I needed to make it my big break again. I desired to be a decent girl, and I desired that goodness be the theme of my life and work.

That narrative captivated me. Can you save yourself? It gave me more power than anything I'd ever known. Realising that we can be conditioned to believe one thing and then be set free to know that things can be different. Fairy tales are usually dark until the light arrives and is earned. I wished to save myself. And I did it. I aspired to be a lady. And, despite the fact that it took years, I believe I succeeded. And I now understand how to teach and embed the foundations of well-being. And that it does not have to be dull. You can be a fighter while also maintaining grace and class. That being free is about liberating oneself. Of course, in full costume. A corset, chastity belt, and a complete turtleneck are all included.

CHAPTER 7

FLOWER LIFE

Aside from "Why are you so much shorter in person?," one of the most frequently asked questions is "How do you do so much?" First and first, thank you for believing I do, but if I do, I feel it is due to the individuals I work with at our firm, Flower.

Flower Films was founded in 1994. We wanted to make movies. We didn't technically participate for three years, but we were permitted inside the process on four films (The Wedding Singer, Home Fries, Scream, and Ever After) so that we could learn how to do things as producers as effectively as possible. It was priceless, and we were pleased that everyone was so forthcoming with us.

Then we got to make our first feature picture, Never Been Kissed. And we sweated over every last detail, and we couldn't have been more invested, and we poured our hearts into every minute of it. It was a success for the studio, but we were mostly relieved since it meant we could do it again. We then watched Charlie's Angels, Donnie Darko, 50 First Dates, Olive, the Other Reindeer, Duplex, Music and Lyrics, Fever Pitch, Whip It, He's Just Not That Into You, and more. We simply attempted to create stories that we genuinely loved and believed in. We tried to keep our heads down and let the work speak for itself. That was everything to us.

We eventually accumulated nearly a billion dollars for our employers. That was yet another comfort. We wanted them to be as pleased as we were that they believed in us.

CHAPTER 8

ADAM

When I first met Adam Sandler, I was in my early twenties. I met him at a coffeehouse in Hollywood because I begged, borrowed, and stole to get him to sit down with me. He was very popular from Saturday Night Live and from his films Happy Gilmore and Billy Madison, the latter of which was directed by my friend Tamra Davis, who confirmed he is such a good person, which is everything.

We had the most fun making it you could ever imagine. And I promise you can tell when people are having fun. It comes out through the celluloid and onto the screen, and it cannot be disguised. Adam's friends who are his team were the best, and I fell in love with all of them, including Allen Covert, an actor, writer, and producer who is in all of Adam's movies, and Jack Giarraputo, his producing partner. We played, we partied, and we became real, no-bullshit friends.

When the film came out, we all rented a bus and went around New York stopping at every movie theatre we could. We would run off the bus, buy tickets, run in, watch five minutes of the film in whatever part it was in at that moment, and then scream, run out, get back on the bus, blast Daft Punk's album Homework, and go to the next stop, all while dancing the entire way!

At the end of the night, when we got to Elaine's, a New York institution, the whole studio was there celebrating, looking at the weekend numbers as they came in, and it was all smiles. The movie was going to be a hit.

And as relieved as I was, I was just happy that Adam believed in me that day at the coffee shop and found us the perfect film to make. I wanted us to be like an old-fashioned movie couple. He was my cinematic soul mate. And maybe I had just proved it to him tonight.

All of Adam, Allen, Tim, and Jack were present. We worked with the same individuals on The Wedding Singer. Adam is a dedicated member of his team. I'm in the same boat as Nan and Chris. As a result, we all feel like family. We understand the value of respect and we all adore one another.

"Instead of Seattle, how about Hawaii," Adam suggested for the film's setting one day. "YES!" we all exclaimed. After each draft of the script arrived, I would give in a batch of notes that all said, "Let's discuss," the next day. Because you never know what will work or not unless you attempt it, especially with comedy. You must not obstruct that process.

And we were developing a film that I actually believed in, with the message "How do you make love stay?" Because, whether someone has a memory or not, you must reinvent love every day. That's why I chose Tom Robbins' book Still Life with Woodpecker as the book my heroine, Lucy, reads every day, because it raises that question and then takes a wild ride, exactly like the film. Love is the one thing that unites and connects everyone. It is what we all desire, battle for, and fight for. And I really liked the version we were telling here in paradise.

We opted to release the film on Valentine's Day, which is when we released The Wedding Singer, since we wanted to maintain tradition. I was presenting Saturday Night Live for the second time, and because Nan and I were producing it, I wasn't as relaxed about the weekend as I had been with The Wedding Singer.

Weekends have become so crucial that they are quite stressful, and you lose some of the feeling of what you intended since, at the end of the day, it is business. Was it successful? Will you be able to repeat the experience? Those are the facts, so those are my questions.

So I didn't want to know the financial figures until Monday. I wanted the weekend to be pure, and the film to be just that: a tale I genuinely wanted to tell. But Adam showed up at his old haunts, Saturday Night Live. He entered the changing room with the entire gang, Allen, Jack, and so on. I raised my eyes to him. He was well aware that I didn't want to know. We made small talk, but the cloud of success or failure hovered in the air like a gigantic rainstorm that would either kill me or cause me to dance in the rain.

The expression in his eye told me he knew what I didn't want to know yet. "Don't you wanna know?" he couldn't help himself. I asked, "Do I want to know?" because his expression was pokerish. with a face that just ate a lemon. "45 million dollars." "We just broke records," the entire room exclaimed. And then I started doing my rain dance, which we all enjoyed. This was one of many beautiful moments. Above all, I felt relieved.

So our movie came to a close, and my new journey began. And I was surprised to learn that Adam and I both have two daughters. It's amazing how life works. We were both kids when Adam and I met. But suddenly we were back at the same spot in our life, albeit a totally different place than where we had started. Not everyone is playing Ping-Pong. We'll be attending our children's birthday parties. Jackie, Adam's lovely wife, and I have a conversation about being mothers.

Adam and I recently found themselves in a corner at Adam's daughter Sadie's birthday party. "What are we going to do next?" I inquired. "I'm not sure. "I've got some ideas," he said. "Perhaps it should be something really crazy?" I remarked to him. And distinct?" But then I considered the heaviness of a drama, and whether or not that would make people happy. I'm not sure. "Well, whatever it is, it's gotta be good!" I exclaimed, and he replied, "We'll find it." We both make jokes about how old we'll be in the next one. We both want to redo On Golden Pond because it takes place on our favourite lake in New Hampshire, which is also where Adam and Nan grew up. It's a small world.

I believe we also enjoy the security of knowing we'll be together when we are very old. Whatever it is and wherever it occurs, I know this... I once knew a young man named Adam. And I hoped we might work together, but what I found was a true partner. I now know a man named Adam, and believe me when I say he is every bit as good as you want him to be.

CHAPTER 8

THE ACTING LESSON

By the age of six, I had figured out the two most fundamental aspects of acting. My mother had us hanging out at the Strasberg Institute in Los Angeles from 1976 to 1983, while she was trying to become an actor. Lee Strasberg was one of the most influential and well-known acting teachers of all time. He and his wife, Anna, were in charge of the school. He had tutored Al Pacino, James Dean, Dustin Hoffman, Marilyn Monroe, and many more modern-day celebrities. At my mother's request, Anna would soon become my godmother, a relationship that would become so crucial to me as a child since she was so kind and nurturing. She placed the mother in godmother and shaped me for the following seven years, largely by allowing me to live in her house and feel comfortable.

Anna's house was like a beautiful commune in that the door was always open and people came and went. There was every famous actor imaginable, as well as great authors and directors. It was a salon-style establishment. There would always be several people watching movies or conversing in the living room. It was the most fluid, creative energy I had ever witnessed in a home. It felt like being in a stimulating heaven. There were also Anna's two sons, Adam and David, who became like big brothers to me and converted me into a bit of a tomboy, which I greatly loved.

After Lee died, I would snuggle into bed with Anna and she would just let me sleep. It was so quiet, and I had the impression that nothing unpleasant could happen there. Anna had lost her soul mate, Lee, and I couldn't fathom how she felt. I couldn't quite get it yet. But I did notice that life continued in this house. I'm talking about LIFE. The house was literally buzzing. It radiated love, fun, and acceptance. A sensation of belonging. This house shaped me, although I wouldn't try to reproduce it until many years later. Now I have my own lovely welcoming home. This was taught to me by Anna.

My mother was doing a play about women in a concentration camp called Playing for Time at the Strasberg Institute in 1979. My mother was cast as one of the camp's women, and they ended up giving me a little part as well. I was supposed to play a female who walks across the stage and says goodbye in German before being led away to be executed. I just had two words for him: "Auf Wiedersehen." Then I waved goodbye, and that was the end of it. This play was both tragic and crucial. These tales have to be told. The primary actress, who carried us through the drama, was a tall, androgynous woman who had to be in the most turmoil every night of the performance. She was crying, shouting, and struggling for her life.

I had no idea how she did it. I was amazed that she could be this emotional every night. What did she do to be ready? What was her ritual, and where did she go afterwards? So I started looking one night.

I'd wander through the empty, darkened theatres with all the ropes and curtains. I'd follow the cables on the floor that snaked about like snakes, powering the bright lights that illuminated the actors. At night, these rooms were terrifying. There are hundreds of empty chairs. Dust and ghosts. A quiet that felt as if anything may jump out and come to life at any moment—like the expectation of a big jack-in-the-box. When a play is in progress, it comes to life. This theatre was now merely a den of mysteries ready to be revealed. But I persisted in my hunt for the wailing woman.

Then I found her one night. I'd gone into another small theatre in the building and hidden behind a curtain so she couldn't see me. She was laying on the stage, her legs dangling over the side. Crying. And she'd pound her chest, conjuring up these massive tears. Then it would calm down a little. Then she'd beat her chest again, moaning as if she was excavating up the ocean floor of her own awful memories. Her weeping, like the waves, ebbed and flowed from a loud battle cry to vulnerable smaller tears. And I understood that every time she walked out there, every time she took the stage, she was already in this truthful-beyond-upset, flipped-out state, and that was what she would deliver to the folks in the audience. But it had come from a very private place within her, one she had summoned next door.

CHAPTER 9

DOMESTIC BLISS

I am engaged. I am five months pregnant. I can't make pancakes. On this particular Sunday morning, I woke up a little cranky. I had a huge zit, and my hair was totally damaged from dyeing it blond, not to mention I was wearing farmer jeans due to my protruding stomach. After sitting in the sun, brushing my hair, and petting the dogs, I came into the kitchen and read the New York Times. And then I had the bright idea . . .

"I know, I'll cook some pancakes." I had just gotten a new recipe for lemon ricotta pancakes, and I thought this Sunday morning would be the perfect time to attempt it.

Cooking has become my latest obsession. I had traded going out to concerts and late-night dinners for a stay-at-home lifestyle. Instead of running around in my thirties like I was still a teenager, I was settling down with my new garden and my new cookbooks and trying to play the part of the character I have never been able to master . . . THE GROWN-UP.

I thought that herb boxes and homemade meatballs were the gateway to maturity. I had an electric pepper mill, which seemed advanced to me! I fantasiscd about being the woman who could whip up anything in her kitchen.

Instead, I now am stretched over cookbooks with a look of concentration on my face with no freedom in my step, still working out a lot of kinks in my very spotty cooking. For instance, my fiancé is puking upstairs as we speak, and it's from my lemon ricotta pancakes. Here's what happened . . .

First I started separating the egg whites. The recipe said to do that, and then whip them into a mountainous shape. So I did. I didn't have a mixer, so I did it by hand and arm. I wanted to cry in pain after ten straight minutes of whipping. But when the liquid started to become peaks, I was thrilled!

Then it said to take four egg yolks . . . Fuck! I threw those away. OK, breathe. Just go get four more. I had now murdered almost a dozen eggs. Not ideal, but I obviously hadn't considered the next step enough, so it's my fault. OK, now I had separated out the yolks, and this time I saved the whites. Not going to be a chump again. Will I need them? Who knows, but in a bowl on standby is better than in the trash.

Step two: Add sugar, flour, and ricotta cheese and lemon zest. So I did. I carefully measured everything like a meticulous baker, and I put it all into a bowl, ready to mix. Fuck. I didn't read that you are supposed to mix the egg and sugar and ricotta, THEN add the flour. No wonder this was sticky!

Feeling guilty about wasting food, I realised that I would have to waste four more eggs to get it right, and do it all over. Resigned to the waste, wanting these to be great for my man, I started cracking the eggs. . . . There were only three. No fourth egg. OK, fine. I would attempt to adjust the other ingredient ratios. Not something I EVER feel comfortable with. Three-quarters is exactly . . . one egg less or a quarter, what? I didn't know how to measure that. OK, breathe again. Be free, I told myself, it's only pancakes. So I trimmed the sugar. I trimmed the ricotta, and, of course flustered, I just started zesting the lemon haphazardly into the bowl.

I started mixing it with the eggs, and to my surprise it was a good consistency. OK. This was all making sense, and the flour should mix with this nicely to make something that resembled batter rather than mortar. Great.

I poured in the flour, and it started thickening. Then more thickening, then too thick . . . FUCK!!!!!!!! I forgot to do a quarter less on the flour. I started throwing spoons.

My fiancé at the time, Will, came downstairs, and instead of finding some sexy brunch-making lady, he found a hissing child. "Don't come near me right now," I said. He has the tendency to want to get involved, and that's the last thing I wanted right now. "I'll be over here," he said as he headed to the couch and started reading the leftover paper.

Standing over the sink, I just felt lost and stupid. I looked at the counters and it was just a giant mess. I sucked in every way and the evidence was everywhere. It was all a sprawling avalanche of every bowl in my cabinet filled with wrong mixtures and flour and spills and splats of eggs and sugar, not to mention the ten spoons and whisks and wooden spoons lying like dead carcasses.

I'm married. I'm five months along. I'm not good at making pancakes. I awoke grumpy on this particular Sunday morning. I had a massive zit and my hair was completely ruined from blond colouring, not to mention I was wearing farmer jeans owing to my bulging tummy. I came into the kitchen after sitting in the sun, brushing my hair, and caressing the dogs to read the New York Times. And then I got a brilliant idea... "I know, I'll cook some pancakes." I had just received a new recipe for lemon ricotta pancakes and decided that this Sunday morning would be the ideal time to try it.

My most recent obsession was cooking. I had given up attending concerts and late-night dinners in favour of a stay-at-home lifestyle. Instead of racing around in my thirties like I was still a teenager, I was settling down with my new garden and new cookbooks, trying to play the role of the character I've never mastered... THE OLD MAN.

I believed herb boxes and handmade meatballs were the ticket to adulthood. I had an electric pepper mill, which appeared cutting-edge at the time! I imagined myself as the woman who could make anything in her kitchen.

Instead, I'm now bent over cookbooks, a serious expression on my face, and no spring in my step, still ironing out the kinks in my shaky cooking. My fiancé, for example, is puking upstairs as we speak, and it's due to my lemon ricotta pancakes. This is what occurred...

I began by separating the egg whites. That's what the recipe said, and then whip them into a mountainous shape. As a result, I did. Because I didn't have a mixer, I had to do it by hand and arm. After ten minutes of whipping, I wanted to cry in agony. But when the liquid began to form peaks, I was overjoyed!

Then it suggested taking four egg yolks... Those I threw aside. Okay, take a deep breath. Simply go buy four more. I'd now killed nearly a dozen eggs. Not ideal, but I clearly hadn't given the following step enough thought, thus it's my mistake. OK, I'd separated the yolks and preserved the whites this time. I'm not going to be a jerk again. Will I require them? Who knows, but it's better in a bowl than in the trash.

Second step: Mix in the sugar, flour, ricotta cheese, and lemon zest. As a result, I did. I meticulously measured everything and placed it all in a mixing basin, ready to mix. Fuck. I didn't realise you were supposed to combine the egg, sugar, and ricotta before adding the flour. It's no surprise that this was sticky!

Feeling bad about wasting food, I realised I'd have to squander four more eggs to make it perfect the first time. I started cracking the eggs, resigned to the waste, wanting these to be wonderful for my man... There were only three of them. There is no fourth egg. Okay, good. I'd try to tweak the other ingredient proportions. Not something I've ever felt at ease with. What is three-quarters? One egg less or a quarter, what? I had no idea how to quantify it. OK, take another deep breath. It's only pancakes, I reminded myself. So I reduced the sugar. I cut the ricotta and, naturally irritated, began zesting the lemon indiscriminately into the bowl.

When I started combining it with the eggs, I was surprised to find that it had a good consistency. OK. This was all making sense, and the flour should combine nicely to form something resembling batter rather than mortar. Great.

When I added the flour, it began to thicken. until there was more thickening, until it was too thick... FUCK!!!!!!!! I neglected to use a quarter less flour. I began flinging spoons.

Will, my fiancé at the time, arrived downstairs to see a hissing toddler instead of a lovely brunch-making lady. "Don't come anywhere near me right now," I said. He has a propensity to want to become engaged, which is exactly what I don't want right now. "I'll be over here," he responded, walking over to the couch and starting to read the discarded paper.

I just felt confused and dumb standing over the sink. When I looked at the counters, I saw a huge jumble. I sucked in every aspect, and the evidence was all over the place. Every bowl in my cabinet was a sprawling avalanche of improper combinations and flour, spills and splats of eggs and sugar, not to mention the ten spoons, whisks, and wooden spoons lying like dead carcasses.

I was going to make this work anyhow. OK. What happens next? So I heated up the skillet and decided to pour or, better yet, thwack my batter into it to begin cooking. At the very least, I hoped to understand what the flavour profile was attempting to express. As the butter melted and the batter began to cook... I detected a pleasant aroma. I received some words of encouragement. These might not be appropriate, but they might be edible.

Now, I should clarify that the last time I prepared pancakes for my husband, they were old-fashioned, blueberry, and raw. He was really gracious about it. But my intention this time was to at least remove that blunder from the equation by just boiling them through.

My current pancake's bottom was browning well, so I flipped it over. It looked great. OK. This time, I told myself, let it cook all the way through. I did. Then I flipped it onto a platter, drizzled it with syrup, and handed it to my little taster. He began with his first taste. I was nervous. And he raised his head and grinned... "It's very good." I was relieved. "And you know I'd tell you otherwise," he added, and he'd be right. As much as I want to murder him when he says he doesn't like something, I am always grateful when he says he does because I know it's true! And I despise yes men. I prefer it to be authentic. Honest. Tough love combined with encouragement! And, of course, when you receive appreciation, it tastes much better! "So, one more pancake?" I wanted to ask because I wouldn't know what to do if he answered no. But before I could say anything, he asked for another, and I cheerfully slopped some more paste into the frying pan. I started getting it right about the fourth one. Size, colour, and preference. But he was already full, and the best of the bunch was on the plate. I gazed down with pride at it, thinking that from now on, I would always give him the later pancakes because the kinks would have been sorted out and that is the quality of service I would like to deliver to my clients. I turned back and stared at the devastation I'd caused in my kitchen. Instead of cleaning up, I sat for a moment, thinking that this should not have taken so much out of me. Breakfast isn't designed to exhaust you physically or emotionally. But there I was, hunched over the kitchen table. I gradually resumed reading the newspaper. Will jumped up from the couch and asked, "What did you put in those pancakes?" with a terrified and pained expression on his face. Oh my goodness, what have I done? "Eggs, ricotta." I began listing things and then asked, "Nothing bad, why?"

"I think I have to throw up," he remarked, and went upstairs to the bathroom. As I sat in the kitchen, wide-eyed, I heard a little voice from the stairs... "I think they were... raw..." His voice faded, as the door closed behind him.

Domestic joy is one thing, but you are not a domestic goddess, I think to myself.

CHAPTER 10

JUMPING SHIP

Mel, full name Melissa Bochco, and I met in 1982 during a John Denver celebrity ski contest in Aspen, Colorado. My mother befriended her mother, and when we went to Los Angeles, where we all resided, she would take me to Mel's house for a sleepover, and then show up three days later to pick me up. This occurred frequently. But Mel and I stayed pals even beyond our childhood. In fact, we're still pals in our forties who have children.

But when I was nineteen, we found out Mel's mother, Barbara, was going on this extravagant boat journey through the Mediterranean, beginning in Istanbul and ending at the pyramids. It was a three-week adventure, and honestly, we weren't at our most sophisticated yet, but we imagined ourselves cruising over ancient ruins and world wonders! On the high seas, luxury? I'm not sure what we were expecting—for me, steamer trunks and old-fashioned movie moments; Mel, I'll never know.

Mel is a salty, sharp-witted lady who makes most people leave with their tails between their legs because she is a cut-you-down-to-size kind of person and, worse, everyone is laughing because she does it with such comedic flair. She has softened with age, and she is perhaps the most sympathetic to people she cares about, but she hasn't completely lost her edge, I'm delighted to say. When we travel,

Mel is known to hang out at headquarters. She's the type of person who would fly to New York for the night, sleep in her hotel room, and then fly home the next day. She sleeps in late and goes about her business. Nonetheless, she's the type of person you want to spend time with. I'm at a loss for words.

So when we learned Barbara was going on this exotic adventure, we begged her to include us. We agreed to pay our own way: I had saved enough money, and Mel would obtain it from her parents as a treat for her mother. Barbara, on the other hand, would quickly come to believe that I was more than just a treat for her.

When Mel and I arrived to meet the group, I had just gotten into my own body, so I was a non-bra-wearing, vintage-clothing-wearing gal carrying a boombox with hand-painted rainbows, love, and clouds on it. I arrived with my serape backpack and super-short blond pixie hair, and I looked like a '90s hippie. Mel arrived at the airport with me, dressed in black, as if every day was a funeral, in roughly 75-degree heat, and I could see Barbara's fear in her eyes from the time we stepped aboard the plane. She knew what this vacation meant to her: a well-deserved once-in-a-lifetime experience at the age of fifty-something, her children finally old enough to rely on themselves, and her chance to get away from it all. Come on in.

On the Lufthansa flight to Istanbul, we appeared to get a similar glance from our flight attendant. Sceptical! Don't get me wrong, Lufthansa is a fantastic airline, but we were being labelled as two young jerks in business class at the time. A sort of "how did you get this seat?" vibe. After takeoff and a few complimentary champagnes, Mel declared to me that she needed to take a "Lufthansa," which means she needed to have a bowel movement, and the laughing went from giggling to screaming! Sneers from the cabin crew again! But you can bet that we still make the "Lufthansa" joke to this day—great airline, again!

We arrived in Istanbul. It was 1994. And, once again, I was simply not dressed appropriately for the occasion. I quickly realised I had completely misinterpreted the dress code. I didn't have anything more fitting in my arsenal, but the minute we walked off the plane, I had that "we're not in Kansas" moment. However, we went outside to meet our greeter who would drive us to the boat, and as I stepped out of the airport, I noticed a massive tour bus. What the fuck is going on? I was a semi-punk-rock rebel of nineteen, and I didn't do tour buses. I also began to count the individuals gathered around the bus, and they were all, at best, Barbara's age. Oh my goodness. Mel and I had entered a senior moment, and we were, to put it mildly, the black sheep. Oh my goodness. So I was already panicking out in my brain as we walked to the bus. I despised well-organised things like this. My style of journey was less corporate and more running nude across fields, but I didn't want to go naked in these regions. That was something I was well aware of!

We were given itineraries, and I was gazing at this dossier with everything planned down to the minute. We were supposed to be escorted through every port and destination. More perspiration. We got on the bus. They transported us to a hotel to adjust to the time zone and explore Istanbul as the expedition's first wonder. That's fantastic.

I felt liberated as soon as we arrived at the hotel. Everything was more calm on this day, and we were able to wander about the bazaars. The senses were ecstatic. Mel and I wanted to explore the markets, but Barbara insisted on going to look at rugs since she wanted an original Turkish rug to take home with her. You're not thinking about worldly belongings and anchoring a room with a memory-filled throw rug when you're nineteen. You're not sitting with friends, drinking tea in the back room of a bustling business, relating the story of how you hand picked this out of hundreds of rugs. But here we were, sitting cross-legged and drinking tea. I simply wanted a beer or something exciting, but Barbara had ordered tea for us, and I didn't want to argue with her. Yet.

The man proceeded to unfurl carpets quickly for almost two hours. He spread hundreds of them out. To keep ourselves entertained, Mel and I began humming circus music. I couldn't discern one rug from another, yet there we sat, stuck, until Barbara eventually chose one. Good! I pondered. We can finally leave now.

I'm sure she was thinking about me, and they began to rise up when we went outside to see the light of day and discovered a pigeon park. Of course, I was a vegan animal rights activist at the time! So, when someone saw a rat with wings, I saw a peace bird! So I began feeding them, and they were so aggressive that they began to fly onto my arms and hands. I was having a great time! The villagers began to gather around me in awe, as if I were some sort of bird whisperer, I thought. Mel speculated that they were probably laughing at me for allowing these nasty things to land all over me. This event quickly became Hitchcockian, and the spectacle of hepatitis meeting an inappropriately dressed American girl enraged the locals. Barbara's little face appeared in the distance as I gazed past the crowd. Yep! She was clearly kicking herself for allowing us to come.

First day. On the water. When I boarded, I saw that this yacht was stunning. It was like a cruise liner, except smaller and more luxurious. I began to feel my own sense of self after paying my own way, and marched right up to my cabin, which I shared with Mel, and unpacked, setting up my boom box with loads of fresh batteries and my case of handcrafted hours-to-make mixtapes, each decorated with stickers and Sharpies and representing a different mood. There was a Cat Stevens cover, a Roberta Flack cover, and an acid-house remix. Everywhere, and each one ready to burst to life to start the party or wind down the evening.

I have no musical talent, yet I have never lived a life without a varied soundtrack. Life is better with music, yet there is one type of jazz that I cannot eat. It's too energetic and spastic to assimilate, more of a birthing of profound inspiration and a hungry call of the wild. This is brought up because I was becoming that for Barbara. I was quickly becoming something she couldn't stand, and every time I walked into a room, it was as if aggressive life-altering jazz had kicked in at level five. We'd get to ten in no time.

We set sail, and I changed into my beautiful white 1940s ruched old-fashioned one-piece bathing suit, went over to the pool, and ordered a froufrou cocktail. I knew they wouldn't question my age because they were more surprised that I wasn't in my golden years like the other passengers. It was more of a "Oh my God, she's young" reaction than anything else. Wait, are you of legal drinking age? So, now that the cocktail cherry had been broken, I determined that drinking would be my lubricant into utter toleration. "This isn't so bad?" I remarked, turning to Mel with my drink. Mel and I cheered as we sailed away from the first port!

We sailed all night and went into the dining area for our first meal. This was a serious white-tablecloth setting. Unlike the older ladies of the boat, I was dressed in a bright paisley Pucci-like dress. Oh my God, this is going to be a long journey, I began to think as Barbara strolled in wearing really sensible clothing that resembled one giant pashmina and we all sat down. Every night for the following three weeks, we were to eat at this table. So, after the first five minutes of talk, I excused myself and went for a stroll.

And, much to my amazement, I discovered a small gambling room! Yes, please! Drinking and gambling! So I started ordering one course for dinner and leaving early every night to hang out with the men at the blackjack table and the roulette wheel. I felt a lot more at ease sharing my experiences with this varied younger crowd, and I didn't feel judgmental. We were all interested in hearing one other's stories. Not to add that I am a die-hard gamer. It was a lot more enjoyable than staring at our plates in the dining hall.

The Greek island of Crete was one of our first visits after days at sea. The stunning Mediterranean scenery absolutely spoke to me. It was fantastic. I noticed the white buildings from a high point on the mountain. And the sea's colour, which cannot be explained because it is both light and dark at the same time! It glistens. It entices. It is magnificent. Today's activity was to travel to the top of the mountain, where the actual town was located, and spend the day roaming around, shopping, and visiting ruins. As you swarmed together, it was like following a herd while a woman gave you the history of this and that. There will be no free-form.

I began to frown. While we were all waiting to go to the top, I noticed people mounting donkeys and beginning their ascent of the winding hills. What? I was too fond of animals to have this poor old donkey lug my a$$ up this massive mountain. So, concerned about this creature's well-being, I declared that I would walk it in protest. Barbara rolled her eyes, ashamed that I would not just follow protocol, and as I began climbing the mountain, the guys said, "Miss, it's too far, you must ride the donkey!" "I'm good!" I said smugly, and murmured to Barb that I'd see her at the top. She reacted with a half-nod, as if to answer but not reveal to anyone else that she knew me.

So, where had Mel gone? On the water. Mel, in typical Mel manner, elected to sit this one out. She stated that there were many Greek islands to visit and that she would do so, but for the time being, she preferred to stay at home. It didn't surprise me, but it was bringing Barbara and me closer together. It was no pleasure for either of us without the Mel buffer. Despite the fact that Barbara had known me my entire life, I was at that unpleasant age for her, and she was not at an age that I could relate to. We had reached a biological stalemate on the Greek islands. She mounted her donkey and rode up next to me. I offered her a hesitant wave.

I arrived at the summit after about an hour and a half. Now I understand why they let visitors ride the burros. My legs felt like they were made of jelly. They were so unsteady that I couldn't walk, and it was the beginning of the day, when we were all supposed to stroll around for hours. Oh my god. I limped around in pain, counting the minutes until we could get back on the boat and I wouldn't have to pretend to be interested in what our guide said. All I wanted to do was take a break and go sit in a café to experience local culture. But I went with the herd, and we proceeded to Crete school.

Fortunately, I discovered a gondola that travelled down the mountain in another region, avoiding the donkey and the arduous ride down. When we returned to the boat at sunset, Mel seemed unharmed and content. What exactly did she do all day? That's what she typically does. Be Mel. Simply slither about like a lizard on a rock. Meanwhile, I was giddy with excitement when I heard the next day's agenda, and off I walked into the casino with my people.

We went to a mosque the following week. Mel had decided to participate on this particular day, possibly due to cabin fever. As we walked in, Barbara wrapped herself in a homemade burka, and I examined my own clothes. Baby T without a bra. Wacky platforms with corduroy bell-bottoms. Barbara and I exchanged glances, and I could tell she felt I was a jerk.

Later, I discovered that the women were supposed to cover themselves, as stated on the day's program. I treated that paper like a wasteful tree killer every morning and failed to learn about the clothing code. So Mel, who dressed as if she was going to a mosque in normal life, was able to cover herself adequately. I wrapped my backpack across my chest, pulled off my shoes, and rummaged in my bag for bits and ends to make do.

I began to cheer up as we entered since I enjoy praying. And here I was on a strange continent, doing something I enjoy in a spectacular setting. I was a student of the cosmos seeking guidance on how to live, whether for the day or for the rest of my life.

Everything had crumbled, but when I opened my eyes, I found Barbara staring at me in my little T-shirt that revealed skin as I

46

bowed down. God. For this woman, I was a nightmare. And a nightmare for the congregation. It was too much for me. I realised I was just someone else's concept of hell just as I was feeling at one with the cosmic fields.

We returned to the boat after leaving the mosque. Mel and I had a lot of laughs, but I was starting to feel down. This carried on for weeks: wake up. Everyone eats together. Take the bus together. We can all learn together. No Mel. There is no pause in the flow of the day's events. And I was too young and foolish to accept the land. Instead, I was mired in the formality of every moment being recorded. It was just not me! I was a captive free bird! It was approaching a tipping point.

The yacht had stopped off the coast one day and simply allowed people to flow freely or simply sit in the pool. I'm not sure why, but this extremely organised group had a "snow day" on the Mediterranean. As I wandered around, instead of feeling liberated, I felt as if this boat being stranded in the ocean was the final straw. I could see land but couldn't get there, and walking about the floating jail wasn't my idea of fun.

Mel recalls that she and Barb were relaxing by the pool when a boatman approached her with a distressed and frightened expression. They raised their heads from their books. "Um, excuse me, ma'am," he said to Barb, "I'm so sorry to disturb you, but your friend has jumped off the boat!" She gazed at him, perplexed, as if he was speaking in another language. "Your friend has jumped off the boat and swam out to that little island, I'm afraid." Clearly, this had never occurred. Barbara's face turned very red. Mel, of course, cracked a wonderful joke—how would they find me? "I suppose we'll take one of the boats and go get her." I apologise; this is unprecedented." Barb received an apologetic glance from him.

And that was correct. Something took over me on the top floor of this massive ocean liner. You know how you get yourself worked up? I thought to myself, "I could make that jump." It's not dangerous enough to kill me. I noticed a very small island in the distance, just a gigantic rock... I could swim that far, right? The elevation. The separation. The idea was too tempting, and with my heart pounding and double-daring me, it culminated in me putting one leg on the railing, climbing, then the other leg, and then I was at the top of the railing and just said "FUCK IT" and flung myself over a hundred feet or so and plunged so deep into the water that I struggled to get to the surface.

But I did it! I broke through and felt alive with that first gasp! The rebel had returned! I quickly began swimming for the distant rock, and after about thirty minutes, I arrived. I dragged myself out of the water, panting and gasping, and I felt that, as much as I was about to die, I had never felt so alive!!!!! Hhhhhhaaaaaaaaaahhhahaaaaaaaaa, you old fuckers!!!! Look who's become the naughty girl!

They all looked at me as if I were the ship's jezebel. The scoundrel who gambles, hangs out with the locals, and looks like a whore from 1972! Now I've proven you correct! Ha!

After the euphoria wore off, I understood in about five minutes that I couldn't set up camp and live permanently on this unfriendly rock. These were the people that drove me home. I sagged in defeat, knowing I'd have to return with my tail between my legs, when I noticed a dinghy in the distance approaching me. I was half relieved and half afraid of having to face Barbara. Perhaps she was correct. Maybe I was simply a stupid, confused adolescent jerk who had made a series of mistakes in my life.

One of the reasons I was excited to attend this trip in the first place was that I had recently married a guy I was dating and was also assisting him with his green card application. The whole thing was a flop, and no matter how wonderful my intentions were, he was a jerk and I was a moron, so we shook hands and filed for divorce right away. I had ruined the sacred character of marriage at the age of nineteen. By the age of twelve, I had ended my career. I needed a significant reboot and had ideas but didn't know how to execute them.

I was still strangely wearing the cheap band that was a temporary wedding ring on my finger. That night, as the boat set sail again at sunset, I went up to the upper deck and gazed out at the water. I was a simple ant in the middle of the planet with a lot to learn. I took the ring off my finger and remembered that you can pray anywhere, so I did.

I informed the gorgeous, colourful sky that I wanted to learn from its all-knowingness as the boat began to enter deeper waters! And, despite the fact that I was lost, I decided to do whatever it needed to find my way! I apologise for messing up my marriage and everything else I might have messed up, but I pledged that I was no lost cause! This strong Almighty didn't give up on me because I was worth it! Please don't give up on me! I hurled the ring out into the pink-orange sky, and it bodysurfed its way into the deep blue sea.

When I returned to the dining hall that night, much to my amazement, the guests thought it was hilarious that I had jumped ship, and instead of turning up their noses or turning their backs on me, they bombarded me with questions about my misadventure. I was suddenly accepted rather than turned down. Even if they're just amused, I'll take it, and with that, I finally had something to talk about with everyone. My AWOL period provided us with common ground, and it was the nicest night on the ship.

I know Barbara was relieved that I was a success! I believe she unpuckered for approximately five minutes and felt pleased about my presence. As in, "I know! She's always been a touch out of control!" "You know, since she was seven, she has always done things her own way," and so on. We ate dinner and then Mel and I went to our cabin. I put on my quiet blues mix, and as Leadbelly's soulful song "In the Pines" came on, we discussed cutting our losses and going early. I liked the concept of going out on a high note. And the next day was the day we finally got to see the pyramids, so as long as I saw that, I was content to cut bait on this scumbag and go home!

As we approached Egypt, I virtually high-fived the old-timers, but Mel and I were quietly planning our escape. We called the hotel and made reservations to get out of Dodge as soon as possible the next day. The boat would continue on, but we decided that three weeks was enough.

We had time to kill after executing what felt like a James Bond job to get ourselves out of Egypt later that night (after the bus journey to the pyramids), so we turned on the television. We changed the channel and saw a Richard Pryor film in Arabic. It wasn't Stir Crazy or one of the others I was familiar with. It appeared to be about him and his family, as well as their "new house." That was all I could think about till the phone rang and it was the cheerful guide calling us to the bus. "OK, let's go see these pyramids we just travelled for weeks to see!!!!" I hung up the phone, grabbed my backpack, and exclaimed to Mel. She was resting on her back, one arm under her head, in the lounge lizard position on the bed, and without looking up at me, she stated, "I'm gonna stay in the room." I glanced at her with wide eyes and a gaping mouth. "What? The pyramids have arrived! This is a once-in-a-lifetime chance! "Are you insane?" I mean, I figured she was, but come on!

She stared at me and gestured with her arm and finger. "I can see them outside the window." My head shook. You could see them out the window because we were plainly in the adjacent-to-the-Sphinx hotel designed exclusively for tourists. "Wow. OK. "I'm out," I said, leaving Mel to watch her Richard Pryor movie in a language she didn't understand.

Mel and I drove to the airport later that night after I returned from staring at those pyramids and enjoyed my renewed lease on life. It was terrible to be two girls travelling alone across the area with all the soldiers and their machine guns. They were inspecting my boom box at the airport and were convinced it was a detonator. I begged and pleaded with them not to take it away. I backed down after being threatened. But they eventually returned it. We waited as the guys with machine guns stared at us as if we were aliens. Our plane eventually arrived. It had been a Lufthansa flight! We dashed into the plane and snuggled into our seats, and I promptly drank my complimentary champagne. As the cabin crew watched us again, I thought, Judge me all you want, but just take me home.

The good news is that we've all matured considerably. Barb was in the front row when I got married a few years ago. I'm hoping she no longer despises me. I'll go on a trip with one of Olive and Frankie's friends one day, and I'm hoping they don't do to me what I did to Barb.

CHAPTER 11

DEAR OLIVE

You are quite intelligent. I know that according to the book NurtureShock, I am not allowed to tell you that you are intelligent, but you are. Let's call it what it is. I've read a lot of books and studied a lot of topics because I've always wanted to approach parenting in a very wise way. In most aspects of my life, I am an overachiever. I take on a lot and demand perfection from myself. I am really critical of myself. And I'm sure some of that is due to fear. And I admit I was worried when you were born because I wanted to make sure everything was just right for you. It all started with your nursery, which is French magazine ready, and my approach to ensuring everything was perfect was very dialled in, from your supplies to asking my sister-in-law for the best babysitters, to making sure the birth plan was all taken care of, complete with hospital room, the best doctors, and your grandparents there and ready.

But you didn't show up. You arrived late. Day after day, I waited. I should have known you'd be teaching me invaluable life lessons from the moment you were born. What is my birth plan? That was not your intention. OK. Got it. You didn't even want to be the astrological sign you were intended to be, so you skipped right into your Libra nest after nine days.

I felt I was going to die from fear during my first few days in the hospital. You were losing weight, we weren't sleeping, and I was sick. Dizzy and absolutely disoriented. When I took you home (the first drive was cliché-worthy, weird, and joyful), it was as if no one else in the world was present. It was just you and me, and all I cared about was keeping you alive.

This persisted for the first three months. I desired complete control over everything. Make every bath the most incredible sound-tracked experience ever. (I believe you are more musical for it, and you enjoy dancing, so that's a plus.) I had been up for days on end. Eating and sleeping were challenging because I was worried about your sleep training, getting your bottle down, making sure you burped, and making sure your room was dark, not to mention the temperature of the room. I could spend all day tinkering with the thermostat. I turned into a poor skit in a comedy show that wasn't even humorous and was more of a study on the collapse of one's sanity.

I demonstrated and explained everything to you. The truck is red. The yellow duck. The cow lets out a moo. By the age of one and a half, you could count to 10. And by two years, up to twenty. It was incredible. On your second birthday, you could name over thirty animals and spell and write your own name. You understand how to express yourself. We also have fantastic chats. You are not in turmoil because you are unable to express yourself fully. (You freak out because, like every other kid, you want more Peppa Pig.)

You've always known what you needed, and, ironically, you didn't need my concern. In many respects, though not on intention, I adopted a survivor mindset. It was crucial to not have a model and to make sure you have consistency, classes, and stimulation. Most importantly, I wanted you to feel secure.

I also attempted to make you giggle all the time, despite the fact that you are a semi-serious bird. When you like it, you like it. Sometimes your expression is "seriously?" and other times I melt you. You burst out laughing and say, "Silly Mommy." It almost has a semi patronising air to it, as if you know I'm being a complete idiot. But I can't help myself. I enjoy making people laugh. For a time, it was even my job. When it comes down to it, I am also a foolish person. You take things extremely seriously, and I can't believe the things you say or the depth of your knowledge of a situation for being just three years old. I'm already up against a mature mentality.

I can hardly wait for you to start school. I want you to go the distance. I will do everything I can to help you on your quest, and I am happy to announce that being an overachiever will benefit you greatly. I know you like having so much knowledge at your disposal, and you make good use of it.

You're still a kid who enjoys watching Cinderella five times over and going on playdates, but you take your art extremely seriously. It's fascinating to watch, and we give you your supplies and stand back and watch you go. It's fantastic. It's also entertaining to watch you read so much and repeat each page out, memorise the books from cover to cover, and even say the writers' names! It frightens me a little.

However, I have no reference. I don't have any siblings and have no idea what the average child development rate is. You just appear to be strong to me. Even when you are hurt, you do not want someone to console you or to hold you. You want to do everything yourself. But, of course, I want to look after you. I try to mimic your beats as well. You are extremely self-aware. And, at the end of the day, you require my strength, not my concern. You appreciate it when I'm really capable and know precisely what to do (it took me a long time, but I'm finally feeling much better).

I volunteer with Seedlings Group and Safe Kids, both of which have taught me a lot. I also discovered a book called Raising Lions, which helped me rediscover my inner strength. I am the primary caregiver. Period. I know I'll have to constantly research, learn, and experience new things in order to be ready for each next phase. But now I feel ahead of it rather than behind it. Actually, I'm looking forward to it. I've got it, and you can always count on me. I guarantee it.

I enjoy being your mother and determining what you require. Even if you need your independence from time to time and don't want me to dance around the room. But I'm not going anywhere. I'll just keep my senses sharp and ready to recognize what the situation calls for, as well as a big armoury from which to draw.

I am overjoyed that you are now grown and robust. You are not a helpless infant. But you're still my cub, and I'll guard you like a ferocious bear. We are both maturing in very different ways. And I am extremely proud of you. You've already surpassed several milestones, and we're just swimming upstream together, holding hands—well, holding hands when you want to, because sometimes you just want to do it without my continual hugs and kisses all over you. I can't help myself.

I love you in such a way that you realise the most unselfish pure love one can have. You are the guardian of my heart. My life's passion. You're trying to figure it all out right now, but I can't wait for you to collapse in my arms and stay for a long time. Forever, in fact.

CHAPTER 12

THE SEAGULL

My name is the Seagull. That's my alias. With envy and interest, I examine other people's dishes. My eyes are like lasers aimed towards everyone's food, which is why: My mother sometimes missed to pack my lunches while I was in elementary school, when I was about seven years old, since she didn't understand she needed to. I was also fed at work, thus this was a genuine mistake and omission. It was normally handled by someone else. Fountain Day School, for example, supplied meals from preschool through second grade. Both hot and frigid. They had macaroni and cheese, canned beets, and black olives that you could put on each finger and then do hilarious hand movements with before eating them off your fingers one by one. Lunch was a joyful time when each child received food and we sat at big lunch tables. There was a cool breeze and it was in a covered place under a roof. It was extremely relaxing. There was peace and order. And because everyone got the same thing, there was no envy or competition. We also wore uniforms, so everyone was on an even playing field.

Fountain Day School was a cute little school in West Hollywood run by a wonderful lady who lived above the property. It was nice there. I felt secure. It was my first day of school, so I had nothing to compare it to. They had a small swimming pool and swim meets. Every year, they would choose one girl and one boy to be the king and queen, which was strange. They would ride blow-up swans up and down the pool's length. It was definitely a taste of jealousy for the ladies. Not only did it satisfy the Pavlovian princess desire, but you also got to ride a swan! I'm not sure what it did for guys, but I do know that our school environment has a significant impact on how we develop. It gives us our first social experiences, which are more than formative. Some are eternal.

Cut to the new format at Sherman Oaks Country School in the valley. It was a world of dog eat dog. Older children. There were no uniforms, and children were defined by their clothing. They were brutal to each other. This was also the beginning of cliques, so you quickly learned your place on the food chain.

In terms of food, the lunch area resembled the Chicago Stock Exchange. The lunacy began when the bell rang. Lunches were commodities packed by parents, therefore there was a strict hierarchy based on who had a finer presentation or greater content. Rachel has a Capri Sun, while Peter has a Ding Dong. Allow the bidding to begin.

It was absolute chaos as each kid sized up each other's meal, and whether someone had a lunch box or a brown bag became essential. (A brown bag was spit on and an amateur; a lunch box was like pulling up in a Ferrari.) Some parents prepare their children's lunches with care. And some parents flung s**t together as if their hair were on fire.

But at these lunch tables, it was all blood sport, with the main game being "trade." "Peter, I'll give you my peanut butter sandwich and some chips in a Ziploc for your Ding Dong?" Jacob, for example, would say to Peter. "In your dreams, you Ziploc-toting piece of shit," Peter would remark to the kid. "If you had a brand-name bag of chips, we could work something out, but for now, keep drooling."

It was disgusting and terrible. Unfortunately, because my mother was not used to serving meals, I was rarely in a position to bargain. I had nothing to barter with, and I would stare at the lunches of these kids because they had something and I didn't. It troubled me less that my father was gone than that I was not participating in the lunch game.

It reached a fever level in my life as I sat there, watching all these kids eat, trade, and work their nasty magic on one another, and it actually affected me. I became a Seagull. Staring gaze. Hungry. Darwinian. I was too proud to beg, so I had to devise a swoop-in strategy to acquire anything. I'd hunt down my victim and sidle up. "Oh, Peter, it appears you're not going to finish that Ding Dong; may I have it?" "Sammy, I noticed you have a turkey sandwich—you know, I've never tasted turkey before." Sammy would simply look at me and say, "I don't give a shit." But I would make it.

Every day, I tried a new strategy with a different kid, and I got my scraps. Don't be concerned. It shaped character. I assume we were expected to have a power struggle. That day, everyone realised what their leverage was. Some days, a kid might as well have generated the Hope Diamond by unwrapping an aluminium triangle and revealing a bit of yesterday night's pizza. Everyone would rush over to begin bidding. It's like Mayhem all over again. Of course, that youngster would either take half of the group's treats or just sit there and eat everything, exaggerating each bite and teasing the other kids. The other youngsters at the lunch tables would go insane with jealousy as he masticated that slice. Heads would blow up.

And the next day, the sick ritual would begin all over again. For years, day after day. I'm convinced this is where the inspiration for The Hunger Games came from. I should find out if she attended Country School.

And, even when I have food in front of me, I observe what everyone else has at every meal, even if I have food in front of me. This lady bought the smoked salmon I had considered ordering before opting for the eggs and sausage instead. When her plate arrived, I could hear the music begin to build in my brain and feel my gaze focus on her plate. It looked fantastic. Goddammit!

I turned to my spouse, and he knew precisely what I was up to before I could even say anything. It's as if I've turned like Lou Ferrigno from The Incredible Hulk, swelling up when I crave food and needing to be calmed down. To this day, I covet, which is why my friends still refer to me as the Seagull. I have that desperate expression in my eyes, but it is pointed rather than sad.

However, there is good news, and the moral of this story for me is that I will carefully prepare my daughter's school lunches. I will work with bento-box perfection. It will be an opportunity for me to do it exactly the way I imagined as a child. It is going to be a chance for me to do it the exact way I would have dreamed of when I was a kid. When I became a seagull in the first place. But don't worry, seagulls are no chumps. And neither am I.

CHAPTER 13

TOADETTE

My partner Nancy and I had always talked about driving across the country. We'd always said to each other, "We have to go on a road trip, and we have to go in an RV." We had fantasies of one of us driving while the other scrapbooked at the table! Sleeping wherever we damn well pleased! Flipping quarters at desolate intersections somewhere in the great USA and saying, "Should we go right or go left? I don't know! Let's flip the quarter!" This was a fantasy we discussed for a few years . . . until one night in 1996.

I called her up late and said, "You know, we can keep talking about this or we can actually do it. And I say we just go rent an RV in the morning and GO!" And much to my happiness, she said yes, and we did just that! Our plan was to go from Los Angeles to Wolfeboro, New Hampshire, where Nan's family had a lake house, taking whatever route seemed fun at the time. We would be on the open road for one month—let the games begin!

We packed our bags, my dogs, cameras, notebooks, and anything else we needed. On our first night we were driving through Palm Springs, and at a checkout stand at the grocery store we heard the checkout lady say to the customer in front of us, "You gonna go see the meteor shower in the monument tonight?" We quickly found out the monument was Joshua Tree!!! We parked our wonderful RV, which we called the Tioga, after the name of the model. We let the dogs roam, and we climbed up the stairs on the back—the ones where, when you're driving behind an RV on the freeway, you think, why are there stairs back there? We lay down on the roof on our backs and stared up at the sky. I took out my old camera and went with a long, long, long open exposure, and waited for something to happen. To this day I have never seen anything like this: All of a sudden, it started to rain stars as if the sky had turned into a shower and the universe was giving us a cleansing from the heavens above! Not bad for night one.

Next we went through White Sands National Monument; Fredericksburg, Texas; all along the southern coast of the country. And a few weeks in we decided, "New Orleans!" I had never been, so why not!

Had we thought it out, we probably wouldn't have rolled in to the outskirts of town in the middle of the night, but being a stupid girl in my early twenties, I just didn't think of dangers like that. And so I decided to pull the RV into the gas station and fill her up. Nan was somewhere in the back; the dogs were sleeping on the bed; it was a typical night in our weeks-long routine. Until the crushing sound— CCCCCCCRRRRRRRRAAAAAAAAASSSSSS HHHHHHHHHHCCCCCCCCCRRRRRRRRRRRUUUUUUUUU UUUUNNNNNNNNNNNNCCCCCCCCCHHHHHHHHHHHHSSSSS SSSSSSSSSSSCCCCCCCRRRRRAAAAAAPPPPPPPPPPPEEEEE EEEEEEEEEEEEEEEEEEEEEEEEEEEEEEEEEEEEE—of ripping metal. I looked up in shock as I realized that I had underestimated the height of the gas station roof over the pumps and lodged myself under it as our RV ripped through the metal overhang!

Oops.

After the loud thunder there was a moment of silence, and I do mean a moment. And then all of a sudden, we heard a shrieking, squawking voice coming out of the glass cashier box. It was distorted due to the fact that the woman was screaming through an old microphone!

Crackling, clucking shrills filled the air! She was yelling words so fast at such a high pitch that I couldn't understand what she was saying. I wondered why she wasn't coming out of there as I moved through the RV to the side door and checked on everyone's status.

61

Everyone was fine. No one was remotely hurt. This was just awkward! SQUAWK SQUAWK SQUAWK!!!!!!!!! The lady screamed again. But why wasn't she getting out?

I opened the side door, and then I saw her. She looked like a cartoon. A very large woman who apparently could not move and refused to try. Crazy wiry black hair and drugstore makeup. She just sat on her tuffet in the glass box, screaming her piece, and her piece finally became clear through the muffled chaos: "I'M CALLING THE COPS!!! THEY'RE ON THEIR WAY!!!!!!!! DON'T EVEN THINK ABOUT LEAVING HEEEEEEEEEEEEEEY!!!!!!!!!!!!!

Shit. OK. No worries. I eventually got a good look at the damage from the right angle, and the scenario was as follows: our roof and the overhang had just merged. They were cats nestled together, and it wasn't evident how to untangle them. Nan and I began to take in our surroundings in all directions as we glanced about... Alleys that are dark. Lit garbage cans! I believe there was tumbleweed! It was obvious that we were in a really rough neighbourhood. I began to panic. It wasn't even the roof that was causing me to shake. I began to worry if the woman in the box couldn't lift herself up or if she was aware that exiting the glass box was dangerous. Shit! I was terrified. Just then, a man emerged from the shadows and approached us.

As he came into focus, he slid from a backlit silhouette to even an odd stringy humanoid with tiny wrists and greasy long hair. The individual appeared to be a guy but was dressed in drag—negligee slip, flip-flops—but the most critical element on top of this pipe cleaner of a man was that he was wearing pearls. Perfect. As he strolled over to us, he shouted his first words, which came out in a long flowing southern drawl: "Y'all better get the fuck out."

As we stood there, unsure if he was a friend or foe, a menace or our newest comrade, he looked us in the eyes. "You ladies really better get the fuck out," he said, moving his hands like an airplane conductor on the tarmac, implying we birds needed to fly away.

SQUAWK SQUAWK, the woman continued to yell throughout the conversation.

"Um, yeah, we're stuck," I said, and he gave me a calm, knowing gaze. He didn't have to say anything like, "Yes, stupid girl, I see that." Instead, he got right to the point: "The cops aren't going to help! You should be afraid of the cops!" This information was absorbed by me. "Oh God," I grumbled. I was now completely enraged!

Nan was in the RV, making sure everything was in order. Licence, registration, etc.—she was the practical one, organising and perfecting everything, while I was the one outside dissolving! The trash cans were on fire in the night, as if someone had set them on fire. The entire scene was starting to resemble Michael Jackson's "Thriller" video! Figures emerged from gaps and from behind abandoned buildings. I dashed back to the RV! "Nan, we have to unlodge this fucking thing!!!" He claims we're in danger, but I think that's becoming quite clear!"

I dashed to the driver's seat and climbed inside. "If I try to get myself out from under this, can you help?" I put my head out the window and asked the unknown individual. He nodded, as if I was finally catching on. My next furious question was directed at him. "What's your name?"

With a Blanche DuBois delivery, he glanced at me and stated... "Toadette."

Without a doubt.

Nan and Toddette took their places outdoors, her in front of the RV and him at the back. I could see her in the rearview mirror and him in the windshield. The dogs were still staring at me from the bed. I depressed the clutch and gradually stepped on the gas. Meanwhile, the woman's squawks became "DON'T EVEN THINK ABOUT MOVING!!!" I CALLED THE COPS, AND THEY'RE ON THEIR WAY, ARRHHHHHHHHHHHHH!" The RV remained motionless. So I exerted a little more pressure, Nan leading the way from the front like a beacon of sanity and Toddette nodding little nods over and over! Nothing! There is no movement. "THE COPS ARE COMING!!!!!" she yelled once more! My heart was racing. I wasn't planning to run from the cops; I just didn't want to be stuck when they arrived. Toddette emphasized the importance of this—"You better get the fuck out"—as though the clock was ticking and the zombies were approaching!!!! Being a sitting duck was a fool's choice, according to the surroundings! "OK!" I exclaimed to myself. "I'm going to stab it!!!" It's on! Anything!!!!! "Be careful!!!"

I slammed on the gas, and the RV lurched forward, and I was out in a flash. I heard a huge tear and looked in the rearview mirror just in time to watch the entire air-conditioning system fly off the top, over the back, and onto the concrete in a perfect rainbow-arching crash, as if in slow motion. Nan and Toddette then ran to it, each taking a side, and crab-walking it through the side entrance and into the belly of the RV, where there was now a huge gaping hole in the ceiling. It felt strange to see Toddette in our mobile home's living room. In a strange way, it's comforting. This strung-out drag queen had transformed into some sort of guardian angel. I got the heck out thanks to his basic knowledge, and it was the first breath of relief I'd had in thirty minutes!!!!

After a minute, the woman in the box realised we weren't fleeing and took it down half an octave, giving us a minute to chat with Toddette. The cops eventually arrived; I wondered what had taken them so long, and then I realised that, despite this woman in the box screaming her lungs out for an hour straight, this is probably not a high-priority case for these officers around these regions. Two morons stopped in a petrol station may have seemed insignificant in comparison to some of the calls these people were receiving. When the cops arrived, I watched Toddette shudder and shuffle slowly backward. I began to feel depressed. Had he simply seen too much? Had he been subjected to such harsh discrimination? What kind of trauma had brought him to these places and this life? He transformed from my new hero to someone I wanted to save.

The cops took our details and sent us to a repair shop for our RV. As they drove away, I turned to Toddette and asked, "Is there anything else you need?" Is there anything I can do to help?" Nan produced some hard cash and presented it to him. She is, once again, extremely intelligent. Toddette would not have benefited from my crisis hotline approach to care. I shiver at the thought of his using money for anything he needs. "Well, thank you very much, Toddette." You truly came through for us." When I heard the engine start, I knew it was time for Nan to get moving.

I walked to the RV, turned around, and saw him slink into the night. He was wearing a lacy slip and flip-flops. Who knows, maybe he'll go out and buy more pearls???

We needed money wired to us from Western Union days later, somewhere in Tennessee—let's just say Cajun Campers had cleaned us out in repair bills for mending the hole in the roof. When asked at a pay phone what name to put the money order under, Nan and I looked at each other and responded, without missing a beat, "Toddette."

CHAPTER 14

KLUTZ

Aaaaarrrrrrggghhh. I just spilled an entire bottle of water all over the counter because I forgot about the cup. This morning, I slid down the stairs. My new stroller (which appears to be back-heavy) collapsed yesterday. Fortunately, my daughter Olive was walking with me; her weight would have steadied it, but it happened as I was leaving this restaurant where everyone was gazing at me—I felt so ashamed. When I turned around, they were all perplexed. I flip everything over. I went on a trip. I fell. I was in tears. I spit. I crack. Why? Will I ever mature into an elegant individual, or will I always be the slowpoke in a hurry? Every two seconds, I find myself apologising. "Oh my God, I'm sorry" or "Excuse me" or swiftly recovering: "That didn't hurt," "I'm OK," "Are you OK?" Where is my head, let alone my eyes, when I step on people's feet or walk into them? Is this how life will always be???????????

I went on The Tonight Show for the first time when I was seven years old, and when I walked out to go up on stage, I slipped and completely ate it. That was perhaps the first time I felt humiliated. People thought it was cute. But I felt deep down that I wasn't putting one foot in front of the other as well as I should. But I had no notion that I would be unable to be cool for the rest of my life.

When I was in school, there was no disputing that I lacked agility as well, as I was always the last person to be chosen for a sports game. I realised what you meant. And, despite the fact that it made me look like a loser, I genuinely agreed with the team captains. You're not interested in me!!!!

When I was a kid, my mother enrolled me in a variety of classes. I couldn't play the piano since I wasn't musical. Tennis—no way, I'm not an athlete. Don't even get me started on ballet. That is a horrible world for girls; it is cliché and difficult, and I despised it. I was short, had boobs, and had no grace, so I wasn't naive about my non-existent career as a dancer. As I previously stated, the only budding in my body was in my chest. Karate was entertaining and, curiously, the one activity I actually enjoyed. I liked how none of the lads in the class made me feel awful about myself. They were just as hard on me, and I enjoyed retaliating. Sparring. Getting new coloured higher belts. I was making progress in karate. I didn't fear getting out of the car to go either. I walked with a spring in my step. I enjoyed battling. I like being tough.

My mother then had me go to dancing class. OK. This was the screw job of all screw jobs. Julie O'Connell, the teacher, and the Julie O'Connell dancers, as we were now known, were compelled to wear spandex unitards—it was 1984, and they were common at the time. That doesn't imply it was attractive. She even produced coats with the words "The Julie O'Connell Dancers" on the back. They were disco-rific, satin with gold writing, and if I could only have one souvenir from those years, it would be that jacket! (If someone finds it, please contact me!)

But Julie would have no trouble comparing the girls in that class as we danced about and learned routines. It was almost as if we were pitted against each other. Later in life, I would become quite protective of girls having each other's backs, which I believe was influenced by some of these situations. Schools and youth might be a time when everyone is learning to swim. Girls understand that they must stick together, but I don't believe that lesson is learned without painful youth isolation.

Anyway, there were always these more graceful girls. Physically, I am more capable. Unitards make you look better. Period. I was clumsy and stumpy. I lacked the necessary moves. The only thing I was good at was kicking and punching. That would come in handy later—I simply didn't realise it at the time. Thank you so much,

Charlie's Angels! And I hoped to one day be a CoverGirl. Then I'll have my own beauty salon. But, once again, we don't know what the future holds while we're young. I've moved on from some things, but I'm sure I'll never get rid of my klutziness.

Aaaaarrrrrrrggghhh. I just spilled an entire bottle of water all over the counter because I forgot about the cup. This morning, I slid down the stairs. My new stroller (which appears to be back-heavy) collapsed yesterday. Fortunately, my daughter Olive was walking with me; her weight would have steadied it, but it happened as I was leaving this restaurant where everyone was gazing at me—I felt so ashamed. When I turned around, they were all perplexed. I flip everything over. I went on a trip. I fell. I was in tears. I spit. I crack. Why? Will I ever mature into an elegant individual, or will I always be the slowpoke in a hurry? Every two seconds, I find myself apologising. "Oh my God, I'm sorry" or "Excuse me" or swiftly recovering: "That didn't hurt," "I'm OK," "Are you OK?" Where is my head, let alone my eyes, when I step on people's feet or walk into them? Is this how life will always be???????????

I went on The Tonight Show for the first time when I was seven years old, and when I walked out to go up on stage, I slipped and completely ate it. That was perhaps the first time I felt humiliated. People thought it was cute. But I felt deep down that I wasn't putting one foot in front of the other as well as I should. But I had no notion that I would be unable to be cool for the rest of my life.

When I was in school, there was no disputing that I lacked agility as well, as I was always the last person to be chosen for a sports game. I realised what you meant. And, despite the fact that it made me look like a loser, I genuinely agreed with the team captains. You're not interested in me!!!!

When I was a kid, my mother enrolled me in a variety of classes. I couldn't play the piano since I wasn't musical. Tennis—no way, I'm not an athlete. Don't even get me started on ballet. That is a horrible world for girls; it is cliché and difficult, and I despised it. I was short, had boobs, and had no grace, so I wasn't naive about my non-existent career as a dancer. As I previously stated, the only budding in my body was in my chest. Karate was entertaining and, curiously, the one activity I actually enjoyed. I liked how none of the lads in the class made me feel awful about myself. They were just as hard on me, and I enjoyed retaliating. Sparring. Getting new coloured higher belts. I was making progress in karate. I didn't fear getting out of the car to go either. I walked with a spring in my step. I enjoyed battling. I like being tough.

My mother then had me go to dancing class. OK. This was the screw job of all screw jobs. Julie O'Connell, the teacher, and the Julie O'Connell dancers, as we were now known, were compelled to wear spandex unitards—it was 1984, and they were common at the time. That doesn't imply it was attractive. She even produced coats with the words "The Julie O'Connell Dancers" on the back. They were disco-rific, satin with gold writing, and if I could only have one souvenir from those years, it would be that jacket! (If someone finds it, please contact me!)

But Julie would have no trouble comparing the girls in that class as we danced about and learned routines. It was almost as if we were pitted against each other. Later in life, I would become quite protective of girls having each other's backs, which I believe was influenced by some of these situations. Schools and youth might be a time when everyone is learning to swim. Girls understand that they must stick together, but I don't believe that lesson is learned without painful youth isolation.

Anyway, there were always these more graceful girls. Physically, I am more capable. Unitards make you look better. Period. I was clumsy and stumpy. I lacked the necessary moves. The only thing I was good at was kicking and punching. That would come in handy later—I simply didn't realise it at the time. Thank you so much, Charlie's Angels! And I hoped to one day be a CoverGirl. Then I'll have my own beauty salon. But, once again, we don't know what the future holds while we're young. I've moved on from some things, but I'm sure I'll never get rid of my klutziness.

CHAPTER 15

GERMANY

GERMANY

I haven't thought about it in a long time, but it still bothers me on a regular basis.

I went to Munich when I was eleven years old to do a made-for-TV movie slash Christmas special called Babes in Toyland—a sort of live-action Mother Goose-type of narrative with a large cast, including a young up-and-coming Keanu Reeves—and we were there for four or five months. We shot on the Bavarian sound stages where films like Das Boot were done, and we lived near Schwabing, a busy shopping centre and beer garden area. I'm not sure how or why I was given such a long leash, but I loved being able to walk wherever I wanted on my own.

There were a lot of individuals in animal costumes needed for the picture, so they hired a number of American teens from the local army base they could obtain at a low price, plus it was summer holiday for the students, so it worked out for everyone. I was overjoyed to be surrounded by a group of adolescents who knew what it was like to move around and live an unconventional life. Heavy metal was alive and well in 1986, and it provided the soundtrack to that summer. Songs from Van Halen, Ratt, and Judas Priest are among those that have coloured my memories. We'd all make mixtapes for each other and trade songs.

When I wasn't working, I would go to places where people could hang out and drink. For some reason, we had no trouble getting alcohol whenever and whenever we needed it. I believe the drinking age was eighteen, and some of the kids were sixteen, and it all sort of washed out.

And that's exactly what we did: we sat about, drank, and listened to hard metal. However, a rock band passed by the motel one night. They were on tour, and I somehow made friends with someone, and we were able to attend their concert. It was so much fun, and after another night of drinking kids, we ran through the hotel and decided it would be funny to pull all the hanging laundry bags full of clothes with labelled forms that listed how many pairs of socks (2) and how many T-shirts (3), and we proceeded to run down the hall yelling with these bags.

To amp up the craziness, we located a bunch of open doors while people were partying in the hotel and hurled the garments down the balcony. There was also a small river below, so some of these people's garments ended up in the water and who knows where they went from there. Other clothes were simply left on the grass and pebbles below.

But we kept going, and I turned to the other kids and said, "Let's go to the floor below and see what's there!" And we all dashed downstairs like we were in the movie Warriors. And there was yet another feast of plastic bags with threaded yarn handles hanging from the knobs of other rooms. We gathered everything in a wild, irrational rage and went upstairs to start tossing again. I suddenly pulled out a pair of sandals and flung one, and then a nasty feeling washed over me, and I wondered, what would this person wear on their feet?—as if clothes were disposable but footwear was not.

My conscience exploded, and I fled to the back of the room, watching everyone as if I were watching it all on TV rather than being a perpetrator and instigator. I was feeling ill. I understood right away that this was terrible, and I despised myself. I don't recall what happened next, but I was soon back in my room, still having a discussion with myself, and swearing that I would never fuck someone over like that again.

This haunts me not only because I will never forgive myself or chalk it up to inebriated, on-the-run eleven-year-old behaviour, but also because my clothing still disappears. I swear to you, if I fell in love with an old T-shirt at a flea market, it will be gone in a matter of weeks, if not months. One by one, my clothing stood up, sprouted legs, and vanished.

My closet has been dubbed "Poltergeist" by all of my pals because clothes appear and then vanish. My one friend Kent suggested that I attach tennis balls to all of my clothes, just like in the movie, so that I can retrieve them when they went missing.

Nothing fit for three years throughout my pregnancy with two children, so I put everything in storage, four to five large moving boxes full of clothes, to make room in my wardrobe. I went in a few weeks ago to get it all out because I'm almost back to normal, minus a few kangaroo pouches and rolls, and all the boxes were gone. Vanished. Years ago, I also lost all of my clothes in a house fire. I'm telling you, I can't keep clothing on, and I'm positive it's because of that night in Munich. And guess what? OK, I tell myself, you definitely deserve it. I am truly sorry and repentant. And I'm confident that whatever I'm wearing as I type this will be gone by the time anyone reads it.

CHAPTER 16

INDIA

I had this recurring dream as a child. I thought it happened in India. I had a feeling. There was no way to persuade me otherwise. I was always afraid of the dream, but I knew it had meaning and wasn't just a foolish vision.

The dream goes as follows: I'm floating above a never-ending desert expanse of goldish sand. In my mind, I'm gliding over it; I'm not flying; it's the view from a tiny pearl-coloured propeller plane. It's an opalescent ship coming in for a landing in the middle of this flat, never-ending desert. The dream then switches to a sight of the plane from the side. It's on the ground, and all of a sudden, the plane's door opens. The kind that folds down and unfolds. Then, roughly ten men dressed in white emerge from the plane. They're all dressed in white, like Indian kurta pyjamas—long sleeping shirts that reach their knees with light slacks below. They're also wearing white turbans. They all exit the plane in a nice manner, single file, and walk to a hole in the ground. The hole is a neatly carved rectangular hole that is approximately ten feet wide and twenty feet long. The men congregate around the opening, leaving the top of the rectangle space empty. The camera then returns to the plane, where one last man exits. He's carrying a golden urn. Then he walks over to the open space and stands there purposefully. The shot then climbs gracefully over the men, glides up and over them, lingers for a moment, and then falls straight down into the pit, fading the entire image to black.

Now that I'm not in the dream, everything I described is exactly what I see, and the dream hasn't altered. What does this imply? I'm not sure. I don't specialise in dream interpretation. And I didn't want it dissected clinically or clumsily by some jerk. This was my private fantasy, which I intended to keep to myself. I was concerned about the entire dying thing, especially because there was a burial-like procedure and an urn. But I also didn't want to claim definitively that the dream was about dying. To be honest, I was thinking, "One day, I'm going to India, and I might die there." But I also understood that my dream would not prevent me from travelling one day.

Years later, I landed in lively New Delhi in the middle of the night! The sounds, the smells, it was the insane mayhem you'd believe was multiplied by a thousand! I was 35 years old, single, and a little adrift in life. Flossy had recently died. I was to meet a man named Shantum Seth, a friend of a friend, who was going to show me around and be my guide. The idea was to avoid any tourist nonsense. We jumped into this dangerous environment. He grabbed my hand, took off my shoes, looked me in the eyes, and down the rabbit hole we went! I had been waiting for this my entire life.

When I was a youngster, I read a lot of religious books and became really interested in Eastern philosophy. Buddhism and Taoism. Animism. Everything was read by me. I was only a beginner trying to figure out how people might sustain the mindset that we are all one. I wanted to think that people had remarkable destinies and that, after all, the majority of our heroes in life are human beings. We may have faith in those people and, more importantly, we can be heroes ourselves. We all have the potential to be divine, yet the ego always allows certain people to believe they are greater or better than others. However, I believe that nature does not decide who is safe or who is allowed to exist. When a tidal wave or an earthquake hits, it's a level playing field. On the other hand, I don't want to get stuck in a defeatist mindset that believes we are insignificant. I must believe in my power to do big things in modest ways, or small things in big ways. To say the least, I was not reared in a religious household. But I appreciate faith. It's great that folks have it. I adore everything that gives us meaning or brings us together. Of course, without judgement.

So there I was, all alone. Shantum led me to numerous sites of worship so that I could learn about diverse cultures and beliefs in their homes, churches, mosques, and temples. There is a Jain, a Sikh, a Muslim, and a Shiva. They all left me in wonder, and I was happy to be able to feel what these places held within them. Several ceremonies and prayer sessions were held in my presence. I'd say a prayer. I'd pay attention. We passed through large boxes of water where one's feet would be washed before entering, but the water was coated in flies—I had to simply get over it and deal, Western girl!

I was back on foot in the city, following the sounds and sights of what appeared to be a funky old Bollywood movie theatre! I've spent my entire life sitting in movie theatre temples. I wanted to sneak Shantum inside one of my churches, so I took his hand and led him in. It was filthy and dirty, with rickety old seats that were a million miles away from Hollywood stadium seating! I had a classic Sullivan's Travels experience as we sat there in the dark, with all the dust particles lit by the projector's light!

In terms of movies, I genuinely believe in the film Sullivan's Travels! Its message is extremely important. It's about a filmmaker who films enormous comedies and feels empty, wanting to make a picture with depth and meaning. So he resolves to go out into the world and seek sadness, anguish, and suffering in order to record them totally and honestly. So the dude discovers it. He ends up in a hard prison as a result of a mistaken identity. After a period, the inmates are given the opportunity to see a movie one night. It is revealed to be a cartoon. The inmates begin to giggle while they are watching. The entire audience bursts out laughing. And he sees the power of making people laugh as he watches them forget about their difficulties for just a while. And then this filmmaker had the most incredible insight! He recognizes that attempting to alleviate people's suffering for a brief while is just as worthwhile as "focusing" on it. His lesson is to deflect someone's attention with a foolish, joyful chuckle. I know there is pain, so being able to escape it for a split second is very empowering. That is one church to which I will remain faithful. The Laughing Church.

We exited the theatre and made our way through the narrow passageways and brightly lit major streets. We went into another place of worship. I turned to Shantum in the cathedral and simply remarked, "I am afraid." He gave me a glance. "I'm thirty-five, and I'm not sure where my life is going, and I'm not even sure what I'm looking for."

And he told me, "There should be no 'I' in what you say, think, or feel." You must distance yourself from yourself. You must understand that 'you' are nothing and 'we' are everything." I enjoyed this and was looking forward to his next statement. "We are all a part of everything," he continued, making an effortless but genuine connection with me. You are the sun, the wind, and a flower in a field. You and I are woven into the fabric of these garments. "Everything is alive and intertwined."

Being a devotee of animism (the belief that all things have a soul) is both uplifting and humbling. I wanted to feel a part of the universe, but for the time being, I was ecstatic about this idea in buzzing, bustling New Delhi. Where there was life and chanting and cooking and vehicles and motorcycles and glorious mayhem!!! They had painted my forehead red at this Shiva temple, and I was wearing a scarf, and I was beginning to shed my Western Self. I wasn't sure what I believed in anymore, but believing in anything that pushes you to go beyond yourself is essential. All of my studies as a youngster were coming together. Following my instruction, the guru and I enjoyed dinner and an auspicious walk through the city! And we ate with joy and comfort. Our energies converged. We had begun the day about two p.m., and by midnight, our legs were exhausted, our bellies were finally filled, and my heart was smiling with all the doors this man had opened. We had finally said good night.

The following day, he guided me through Transcendental Meditation. Three hours with your eyes closed and no movement permitted. Travelling to anyplace you desire to go in your imagination. I must admit that I felt really uneasy for the first hour. I went from an enthusiastic student to "let me get the hell out of here NOW." My legs hurt, my back hurt, and I was irritated. I may have agreed to it, but I wanted out. I'm not sure what kept me in, probably pride, but I stuck with it. And as I resented him for putting me in something too complex for a valley girl like me, I saw myself as a bird. What kind of bird would you like to be? I questioned myself. A bald eagle! So why not? Let's get majestic, I reasoned. As a result, I took off. I began to fly as I soared higher and higher. My legs suddenly stopped hurting so terribly. And I flew over New Delhi. Then there was India. Then I remembered all the locations I wanted to visit, and everything seemed limitless and full of possibilities. It was incredible to fly over the entire planet and spy on pals. Most importantly, it showed me that we are not bound. We have the ability to go anyplace we want, whenever we want. Following that, I had dinner with Shantum's family, eating his wife's meal and playing with his two girls. It was so cosy in his house. I may have pondered where my life was going, but for the time being, living in India was ideal.

After that, I boarded a plane and flew to Bhutan, where I spent a few weeks travelling throughout the nation before returning to India for a time. When the time came for me to return home, I began the lengthy journey at the airport in Rajasthan. When they announced our flight over the loudspeaker, the other passengers and I stood up and made our way outside to the plane.

Okay, here we go...

When I stepped out onto the tarmac, there was a small pearl-coloured white propeller plane sitting there... just like in my dream.

I was literally paralyzed after I stopped walking. So that was the end of it. It's crunch time. I took a look around. The sun was setting as the last flight of the day took off. When I say sunset, I mean golden movie hour. It's God's time. Nature strutting her stuff! It was pure gold!!!! This was the predicted scenario I had pondered my entire life. I took a long chalky breath and made the decision to confront the wide unknown. My knees were shaky, and I was dizzy. What in the world was I doing???

As we began to lift off, the engines roared. The passage of time had allowed the gold of the sun to set to its most exquisite pink. Similar to a vacation drink. The inside of a seashell, or blush... It was as beautiful as anything I'd ever seen. Of course it will be picturesque!! I might be going to die!

We departed.

And as we rose into the sky, I looked up at the sun, my eyes burning and my throat hollow. My heart was racing and I was in a state of terror. All the meditation in the world wouldn't help me right now. I appeared to be an animal who had accepted its fate. Wide-eyed! Trembling. I began craning my neck, hoping for the bar cart, knowing full well that they don't serve drinks during takeoff. Oh God! My seat was genuinely shaking back and forth. The motion was either going to calm me down or make me dizzy enough for me to pass out. I was a walking advertisement for Xanax!

I took another glance out the window. I sat there, silent, astounded by the spectacular beauty of the sunset. The silence allowed me to consider: What if I had a second chance at life? What would I do differently next time? What would I keep and what would I throw away? My older self was ushering in my younger self as a young woman. This was not the death dream it had appeared to be for all those years. It was a new beginning. I learned right then and there that you have to work hard in life to make your aspirations come true. Even if it's just the ones you need to find out. I went from afraid to hopeful. The plane and I both levelled off.

CHAPTER 17

POST PARDON ME

I'm braless, not in a sexy-activist sense, but as a sexless shloomp who rationalises sweatpants as a uniform rather than a snug private luxury. I am a mother of two daughters. Olive is three years old, and Frankie is one and a half years old. I am a hands-on, overachieving mother who also works. I also have a wife. None of this is in any particular order because anyone with these obligations understands that it is a juggling act. Even the phrase "balancing act" does not really describe the circus that is attempting to perform all of these things. I've gotten into problems for saying that women can't have it all. If you truly want to raise your children, something has to give since it is all-consuming. It is not necessary to give up everything. That is wonderful news.

But you can't accomplish everything all at once. Being a mother entails making sacrifices. Putting someone else ahead of yourself. This covers one's schedule and job load, as well as play mode, sleep mode, and creative-juices mode. It was difficult to regain inspiration after having my children because all of my thoughts were focused on them.

I recall being unable to think about work after having Olive. It irritated me. Work seemed like a horrible man luring me to cheat on my children. Or I just couldn't take anyone seriously, as if they were insane to think anything was more essential than keeping a child alive!!! "Are you sure? Does that have to be done immediately? "Well, you're an idiot for caring," was my internal monologue whenever anyone attempted to discuss work with me. I simply didn't care any longer. That was liberating for me because I had been a workaholic my entire life! But it was also frightening because I needed to earn a living in order to raise my children, and I wondered if I would ever want to work again! Will the pleasure or motivation ever come back?

I devote the majority of my time to my children. So when I set aside time in my day or week to work, I am conflicted. It takes me hours to disengage from my laser attention on my children. Then comes the guilt—"I should be with them"—and unless I've pulled off a five-day marathon with them on my own, I never leave the house without feeling like a horrible jerk! I know I'm not the slacker parent I'm beating myself over! I am a crazy, involved, caring mother! Obsessed with my priorities and being in the correct spot at all times. I would do everything for and with my children.

But every now and then, when I'm at the pony park or the bouncy-ball place, there's a little miniature devil on my shoulder yelling "You have to give an hour or two to work!" and I feel bad because I didn't work hard enough that week because I didn't want to wake up my kids! I'll get them breakfast! Bring them to their weekly music and painting classes with me! Men, it appears, do not do this to themselves, and women are simply insane when it comes to parenthood.

Speaking of males, some of the mommy-and-me groups I attend are like a penis-measuring competition to see who is the most involved mother! I swear to you. And then I begin to reject it! I can do anything by myself, but in a group setting, I rebel. I'd rather sit at home with my kids, play with Play-Doh and glitter art, and order pancakes from "Olive's store" than compete with anyone. As much as I want to be the finest mother in the world, I don't feel like I fit in with the pushy mommy clique. But I know we're all working together to get it right.

When I returned to work directly after Frankie, the battle appeared to reach a peak of agitation in my thoughts. I did not receive the traditional maternity leave. I went right back in and made a film, which is what I've struggled with the most. And even though I had three-day weekends, I still felt like the world's worst mom, and I decided to take even more time off acting. I was already limiting myself to one or two films every year or two. I even took a three-year break. But now that I'd relocated the family to London, I was dealing with postpartum depression for the first time.

That was not the case with Olive. I felt the "everyone is stupid for caring about anything, and I don't want to do anything but be with my baby" mentality. But finally, like in slow motion, sound returns and the focus returns, and you begin to place one foot in front of the other. "Oh my, I actually just had a creative idea," you say. Alternatively, "I made a phone call about something." I started becoming involved again, even though life goes on without you, and I was nervous about stepping back in and wondering if I had anything to offer. It took some time—I compared coming back to work after having a baby to physical therapy after an accident. One step at a time, working toward some form of rehabilitation but knowing that nothing will be the same.

This time around, with my second child, I felt like a failure on every level. I wasn't also attempting to make everything perfect with just one child. I was trying to keep my oldest happy and make her feel like she was number one while an invader to her throne crawled around. Was I doing enough for my new child? How much do I just listen to everyone when they say that it's most important to make the older one happy because the smaller one isn't aware of what's going on? Really? since my Olive is Miss Independent and my little one is a "stage-five clinger" who cries if I even leave the room, which I love since Olive is strong-willed and wants what she needs just when she needs it, and Frankie wants all the gooey love I have. My children appear to need me equally, even if their needs are different. So, unless I transform into a human octopus or slice myself up like a pizza, no one will get my best. I'll just attempt to do everything, but I'll do it poorly and with anxiety.

So I kept working on the film because I had committed to it, and I gave it my everything, but I noticed that my typical Labrador acting style wasn't there because I wasn't completely present. I was suddenly older, and it was beginning to show in my performance. I'd done a bunch of romantic comedies, which were enjoyable, and then Grey Gardens, which required a very different degree of dedication. I shut off the world for four months in Grey Gardens to actually become this symbol, but with where my life was at with a family, I realised that would never be feasible again. All of a sudden, I felt like I was doing something less infantile and desperate in my performance. Not to dismiss what I've done, but there was always a childlike quality to my art, and all of a sudden I was a woman who could take it or leave it. I was relieved that this was different.

I decided to do this because my husband, my business partner Chris Miller, and my agency Peter Levine all advised I should. Three men I admire. The irony is that, while being a female-centric film, it transcends and reaches others because it's a beautiful story about two lifetime best friends. And one is attempting to conceive, while the other is dying of cancer. So the entire cycle of life depicted in this love tale between these two women is so poetic and powerful that I wanted to be a part of it. I turned the pages of the script with Frankie in my arms and Olive in her high chair when they handed it to me to read. Because it was so emotional, I would make breakfast for them while sobbing as I read one page here and one page there. I explained to Peter that I didn't even have time to read this—how was I going to do this?

And he and my spouse promised to assist in making it happen, so here we were. Toni Collette, my co-star in the film, is a woman I greatly respect and adore. She has given some of the best performances of our generation, in my opinion. She was Milly, the cancer patient, and I was Jess, the lady striving to get through everything in order to establish a family. I was supposed to be pregnant for much of the film as well, and having just had a baby, it worked out perfectly.

But, more importantly, I kept wanting to be a part of this since all of the ladies in my life have lost someone close to them to cancer. Nancy, my sweetheart, lost her mother. Coco, my mother-in-law, lost her mother, her hero and best friend. "I am so proud of you for doing this," Coco exclaimed after Coco read the script, and I felt like a little girl who had done something good. It was the kind of adulation that kept all the monsters at bay.

Surprisingly, my personal mantra comes from The Simpsons. There is an episode titled "And Maggie Makes Three." In it, the entire family is browsing through a photo album, and there are images of Marge, Bart, and Lisa, but there are no pictures of Maggie. As a result, it narrates the account of how Homer was dissatisfied with his job at the power plant. He worked in an octagonal room every day, staring at an Orwellian plaque that stated, "DON'T FORGET: YOU'RE HERE FOREVER." When Homer returned home one day, he informed Marge that he was terrified of his entire life slipping away without him ever getting to live his ambition of owning a bowling alley.

So they all scrimped and saved to make it work, and Homer eventually got his dream job! He became so thrilled that his hair began to grow back! His life was falling into place with his wife and two children, and then Marge became pregnant. Of course, in order to provide for his family, he had to return to work at the power plant. And he did just that.

The youngsters, however, reply towards the end of the program, "Yes, but why are there still no pictures of Maggie in this photo album?" Homer replies it's because he puts her images where he needs them the most, and the scene shifts back to his office, where they're all pinned up on the plaque in front of him for inspiration. However, the manner he has put all of Maggie's images on the plaque has obscured some of the wording, and it now reads, "DO IT FOR HER," which he now sees every day.

Do it for her sake. That's all there is to it. You demonstrate your undying devotion for them. You invest your time. You make a sacrifice. You also teach by example. The way you live, what you do, and how you behave will be more visible than any attempt to persuade people of anything. I alternate between being a stay-at-home parent and a working mom. But, first and foremost, I am a mother. When we mothers worry, guilt-trip, or try to convince ourselves that we will never be the same again after having children, we are missing the point. We will not be the same. I feel as if I was born on the same day as my children, and that my existence before that was simply for the purpose of gaining wisdom for them. The point is that you give it your all. Every day, give it your all. You do it, and it's for them!

CHAPTER 17

THE ROYAL HAWAIIAN

When I was about two years old, I met my grandfather for the first time. Shuni was his name. He and his second wife, Marta, lived in Pennsylvania, which was my mother's home state. My mother was not born there; she was born in a German wartime displaced persons camp. Shuni met Marta there and left his wife—my grandmother and my mother's mother—to live with her. But, according to my mother, the marriage had ended long before that, and the camp had forced my grandfather to reconsider. He wanted to be happy, so after they got out, the family moved to Pennsylvania, and then everyone went their separate ways.

My mother's upbringing seems to have been incredibly dismal and bleak. Her mother was unkind and eventually bitter as a result of her life not going as planned, and she took it out on everyone around her. I don't even know what her name is. I met her once when I was very little, and I remember my mother being quite guarded and stiff around her. It was air that could be cut with a knife. That's all I recall. One unpleasant interaction.

However, I adored my granddad. I knew he was a wonderful person deep down. Interesting. A fantastic artist. He was a stained glass artist who could draw brilliantly. My mother could, too—she was incredible. I've never dared to draw before. It reminded me of her, but I believe the talent was passed down through generations. But I was glad since it set us apart, though I'm not sure if my daughters will have that skill.

My grandfather John and great-uncle Lionel were also talented artists, so it runs in the family. John wanted to be an artist before the family business of acting swept him up, but he always felt that he didn't get to draw his way to fame as he did onstage. If I see a talent in my daughters, I promise to nurture it. It's remarkable how someone can express themselves via their hands and make it beautiful at the same time. Sometimes I suppose I'm attempting to paint a different picture of my own family in my own unique way. One in which everyone remains in the frame.

Despite the fact that my grandfather Shuni lived across the nation, we all made an effort to see each other. He and Marta would come to our West Hollywood duplex and stay for a week or two.

I recall him taking me to Grauman's Chinese Theatre to see my grandfather John Barrymore's hands and feet in the cement among all the other cinema stars', only John had also put his face in there because he was regarded as "the great profile." I liked how he was unusual and had gone for it.

As one grandfather educated me about the other, the other grandfather assisted my father. My father once broke into and damaged our house while Shuni was living with us. He shattered all the plates and pulled everything apart, and even worse, he stole the secret spare key. My grandfather volunteered to get it back from him because he didn't want him to have access to our home whenever he felt like venting his rage. A meeting was set up for the two of them. My father came flying around the corner to pick him up (where my father obtained a car was a mystery, since he didn't own a home, didn't wear shoes, and certainly didn't have a car!), and he drove up, and we witnessed my grandfather step out, get into the car, and then it ripped down the street and out of sight.

We all hurried to the window, which was louvred glass slats, and saw my grandfather get out of the automobile, obviously inebriated to indulge my father, and come up to the home. The automobile zipped away again at breakneck speed, and as my grandfather went in, he composed himself, smiled, and opened his hand to reveal the key.

We travelled to see them in Pennsylvania on our next visit. It was my first experience with snow. My granddad was one of my favourite people because he made life fascinating. He'd explain how snow formed and how it works. He would explain the functions to me, yet nothing lost its poetry.

I believe my granddad made me believe that everything was magical. We spent the entire day playing in the snow, and he handed me Peanut M&M's to give to the squirrels. With a gleam in his eye, he gazed at me. "They love it," he says. And he was correct. They went bananas for them. His garden appeared to be a little, icy-powdery world where creatures ate candy and everything was safe and beautiful.

I was always calm when I was with him and so sad when I had to leave him, so I was overjoyed when my mother pooled her winnings from making E.T. and took us all to Hawaii.

It was my first trip away from home. Because the film had not yet been out, I had not yet travelled around the world for the E.T. press tour. It was 1981, and it was the last time my life felt easy. We stayed at the Royal Hawaiian Hotel in Honolulu. The motel is completely pink, a lovely bubble-gum flamingo pink. Pink, like many other ladies, had a Pavlovian response in me, and I adored it. It was right on the lake and looked like paradise; in fact, it was my first taste of paradise. When we stepped off the plane, the hot air and floral scent immediately transported us. When we landed, I knew we were in a different place. It's so open and airy, and I couldn't be happier.

We all set up camp and spent our days on the beach or doing fun kid-friendly activities like snorkelling at Hanauma Bay, where there were so many fish that you could hold a stack of saltines under the water and, as they disintegrated in your hands, a swarm of fish would swim up and nibble the crackers right out of your fingers. It was a thrilling experience that I couldn't get enough of. I returned home exhausted. I wish life could be like this, but I guess that's why it's called vacation.

I didn't get enough sleep at home. I was stressed and had trouble sleeping. Even to this day, that has always been a significant telling indication for me—where do I sleep peacefully? I don't even feel that comfortable in my own bed due to everyday life concerns. But every now and again, somewhere will wrap me and literally throw me into a deep, easy slumber, and those locations feel so wonderful to me, and regrettably, rare. One of such places was Hawaii.

I enjoyed walking around the hotel grounds during our days in Hawaii. Palm fronds would cover my path, and I'd find myself travelling to see my grandfather in his bed. He was always doing something, whether it was reading, drawing, or writing. He was a deep thinker. When I came in one day, we were discussing human anatomy, and he was shocked to realise that I didn't recognize my knee from my ear. I just didn't understand how anything worked or why it was there.

He gave me a glance. "Did you ever wonder why we breathe? Do you understand what bones and muscles are? Do you know how we grow hair and why it only grows in certain areas?" I fixed my gaze on him. "No, no, no, and no." I honestly didn't. Nobody, not school or adults, had ever explained the simple or sophisticated workings of anything.

So he decided to build me a human body chart right then and there. Once again, if you can sketch something, you can accomplish anything. And while he was doing that, I sat on a chair, enjoying the breeze that was blowing through the window. Then I noticed the minibar in the corner and crept over to it, opening it quietly. I discovered a chocolate and begged him to give it to me. My mother was a health-conscious vegetarian who would never accept such things. She was a part of the 1970s health-nut hippie movement. I don't think I'd ever tried chocolate before. I stared at him, and he nodded softly, just like he did with the squirrels. He knew it was a treat and that treats were good in life.

I unwrapped it and turned to face him. He observed me taking a bite while my thoughts were exploding. I gave him a kind grin. He grinned at me before returning to his drawing. I know he was relieved that I was having a good time. And I learned a lot from our unspoken conversation. He thought that people should do activities that make them happy. Perhaps this is why he eventually left his wife. She was considered to be really chilly and harsh. Perhaps he realised that life was short and that feeling well was essential. Perhaps this was not simple for him. Perhaps it weighed so heavily on him at times that he was unable to stay. But he was someone who could detect happiness. And other people, no matter how hard they try, simply cannot.

CHAPTER 18

NUMBER ONE

Liza intimidated me when I first met her. My best friend Robin introduced us, and I would accompany them to lunch, but our ages were so different that I didn't completely relate to the talk. Liza was ten years my senior, with two girls between the ages of eight and ten. She had a husband. Mature. But that's fine. She is a powerful executive who is responsible for several films that are nominated for Academy Awards. She has excellent taste. She is capable, but when I was twenty-eight years old, she was terrifying. But we shared a best friend, so I'd go to her place for meals, and there was a great bohemian crowd, with a chef, and her husband, who you could see is brilliant and has a great taste in wines, so I'd just hold out my glass and drink different wines all night. I wasn't married with children and had a long way to go before that happened.

Years later, Liza and I collaborated on a film she was producing called Big Miracle, a true story of a Greenpeace activist who set off a series of events when she attempted to save three grey whales in Alaska. The White House, Russia, energy firms, and the world media all got engaged, and for a brief while, everyone put their objectives aside and really worked together. It was an excellent and engrossing story.

As a result, Liza and I got to know one other in a unique way. I was thirty-five years old, single, and had just returned from India. For a long time, I avoided partnerships because I knew I wanted things to be different. As women, we are aware that we have a biological window within which we must question ourselves, "Do I want to have a family?" I knew that no matter what, unless I made significant changes in my life, it would not happen in the way I expected for myself and from myself. I was still young in relationships, if I had grown up at all. A working woman who is also a child in love. It was time to reorganise and clear the decks. Allow room for a large, profound, life-changing love.

Liza and I would sit around and discuss it. I was in my "I'm not ready" attitude when we first arrived in Alaska. "I just don't know what's going to happen," I'd reply dismissively, "but I don't even know what I want to happen." I was fatigued from spending so much of my life worrying about someone else. And then I was alone, working in this snow-globe-like atmosphere in the middle of Alaska. I was reading novels again after returning from India; I had adopted another dog, Douglas, a frightened mongrel with chopstick-like legs but a decent snuggler anyway; and I had discovered football and was obsessed with it. It's amazing what you can do when you're alone. It's actually a lot of fun.

Midway through the film, two months later, I had physically cooled off on the ice floe where we shot every day, and I found myself telling Liza, "You know, being single is amazing! I'm not sure why we approach it like a disease that needs to be cured with a 'where is he' remedy, since I don't want to know where he is all of a sudden. This is fantastic. "I enjoy being alone." She grinned as she glanced at me. Since my arrival, I've definitely changed my tune. At first, I was depressed and sceptical. And suddenly I was feeling possessive about my life and my place.

When the movie ended, I had a new feeling of self. Something had completely changed in this town of Anchorage, and I was overjoyed. I knew myself in a completely new manner, and for the first time, I felt like a full person. Someone else does not define you. When I left Alaska, I'd go to Liza's for supper with a new sense of belonging. No, I wasn't married with children yet, but I wasn't a child either. I'd drink wine with Liza's husband, Matthew, and talk to her other visitors with a newfound sense of maturity or perhaps a sense of serenity I'd never felt before. My life had calmed down, and I wasn't a workaholic, which was good for me, and I wasn't with a man, so all I had to do was analyse myself and become completely comfortable without any distractions. I could feel the next major step approaching.

Will Kopelman and I had met a few years prior, in 2008. We met at a friend's house, and he asked for my phone number, which I appreciated because I thought men no longer did that. In contemporary society, women were frequently the aggressors, which changed the ancient evolutionary courtship of thinking the lady on the head and dragging her back to the cave. Which I was starting to miss because I felt like men assumed we didn't want to be chased anymore—of course, we'd come too far, which I respect, and I don't want us to go back in time, but I was tired of being the one who had to make it happen. So when a man asked for my phone number, I nearly fell out of my chair. I was delighted by the old-fashioned inquiry and promptly answered it for him. Of course, he waited two days before calling.

We had a great time dating for a few weeks and had a lot of fun. But it was only for fun because we were both in the wrong place at the wrong time. So we just went back to our lives, and that was the end of it. But it was so lovely. And getting to know him was a total joy. But "timing is everything," and I couldn't be more enthusiastic about that universal clock that you can't control since it knows when things are intended to happen better than you. And in this new phase of my life—I had been sleeping alone for nearly a year, sleeping in the middle of the bed, and really working on myself—I began to be concerned about meeting someone because I was feeling quite differently than I had ever felt before. I was so strong, and I didn't want anyone to take it away from me. Someone had to be the human equivalent of an addition rather than a subtraction. Period.

It's odd that we rush through being "single" as if it were a disease or adversity to be cured or overcome. The truth is that you will most likely meet someone and then they will disappear. And once it's gone, it's gone forever! Why doesn't anyone tell us how vital it is to embrace being single and alone? That period is defining and magnificent, yet there is nothing to "cure." Being alone will actually prepare you the best for being with someone else.

Then, one night in 2011, I went out with my business colleague Chris Miller after an event, and because we were all dressed up, we decided to go out and have a nightcap. I was trying to catch the bartender's attention when the man in front of me—whose shoulders I couldn't see past, despite the fact that I was hovering—turned around, and I instantly began to apologise for being in his space, when I saw it was Will Kopelman. Oh. Hello. I looked down shyly.

Something happened right there and there. Here was this cute pleasant man, whom I knew well enough to know was a wonderful person. The training wheels were removed, and he no longer appeared to be amusing. He appeared to be genuine. When Chris turned around and muttered "Oh my God," the feeling in the air was palpable. Will was with his buddy Diana, and Chris and Diana must have done some sort of recon because Chris went over a few minutes later and enthusiastically whispered in my ear, "He's single," and smiled at me before sashaying away. Maybe the timing wasn't off any longer?

We went on a few dates that were incredibly enjoyable but also relaxed and free of games. There was goodness there, as well as a startling trajectory in which everything seemed to come into place. As my date for my birthday. Getting to know the parents. Travelling. Everything was well because my buddies liked him. I loved bringing him to my parties since he was classy, could hold interesting conversations with people, and was consistently amazing.

I began to panic. What about my newly discovered sense of self? Is that anything that has to go? Would sharing a life imply that I was no longer my own person, but rather a "we"? How might I remain one of two instead of becoming half of one?

I began to scrutinise everything, as anyone who is going to settle down would. I asked Liza if she and Matthew had any Passover plans around that time. Given that Will's family was in New York, I was attempting to take him to a special place to celebrate. Thankfully, she welcomed us right in, and we were off to enjoy some fantastic wine and a delicious Seder.

I simply adored the atmosphere of their home. It's cosy but active. People speaking, food being prepared, and familiar faces. I was bathed by warmth, which soothed my pent-up state of pondering how this love with Will might grow and justify progressing to the next level. You don't wait years at the age of thirty-six; you review the relationship after a few months so you don't squander years and then find yourself without certain options. Although I am with men when they desire to escape the stress of a woman's biological clock! I understand.

However, this is biology, and these are the facts, so when you consider becoming very serious with someone, it is serious. I hoped you'd be back to having fun soon.

Of course, when Liza inquired how everything was doing, I spilled the beans, in another typical girl cliché. I mentioned that we were really considering going serious, but "how do you know when and how you should get serious, and why does it all feel so serious?" She could see the fear in my eyes. She grinned coolly and knowingly, chuckled, flung her head back, and then peered deep into my eyes. She said, "Door number one."

I looked at her, perplexed. "Excuse me," I inquired. "Everyone wants to overthink and analyse and take all the fun out of it and freak out," she continued, "but the truth is you choose door number one." You choose the amazing individual in front of you rather than playing Let's Make a Deal and seeing what's behind door number two because we are so conditioned to seeing what else is out there."

"I thought you were talking about Let's Make a Deal," I said. "That's right," she confirmed. "You're so lucky because he's right there." She pointed to him, and there he was, my responsible, handsome date, engaging in pleasant conversation with my companions once more. I returned to her with pride and tranquillity. "He is fantastic. And he is the first door. And I'm aware of it. And he's standing right here."

"And you know what's behind door number two, of course?" she replied with a smile. I asked her a question, and she replied, "A donkey and a broken washing machine." So just do it. Go make this happen. Will is the first door."

And she was correct. I didn't doubt that he was "the one." I was trying to figure out how I was going to go all the way with this man and truly create the family I had always desired. Liza was also stating that there is no time to look back. You make the decision to commit and proceed. You go about your business. And you value what you have.

That's all! It's the best advice I've ever received. I was smitten. I have two lovely girls who are my entire universe and for whom I live my life. And if you are fortunate enough to be given the best opportunity, seize it. Keep it safe. And don't give up. You can also get a Kenmore. Or you might be a jerk.

The first door. Thank you very much.

CHAPTER 19

DEAREST FRANKIE

You are the most delectable little girl, and this is all I have to say about you...

I had planned a music for the delivery room when you were born. I put nothing but Billie Holiday on it. It's such soothing music, and hearing it immediately transports you to a timeless, tranquil place. (I believe this is why so many people, including me, wear it to dinner parties.) I knew her music's tranquil state was great for the vibe I wanted to create, and when you were ready to go out into the world, the last song stopped and the next one began. The song was "God Bless the Child," and the entire room began to swoon. We were all aware that the timing couldn't have been better. What a marvel!

And there you came, and as I lay there waiting for you to be placed in my arms, I heard your father remark, "Oh my God, she looks just like you," and of course I waited to see what he meant. You were placed in my arms, and I simply clutched you as if I wouldn't let go. We were finally together, and even though I was dizzy, I just grabbed you and looked at your face, making sure you were comfortable. Your lovely little face.

We were escorted into the recovery room together and stayed there for the following four days. Olive came in and offered you a gift, a small plush bear, while keeping a close eye on you. As I snapped a photo of you two, I thought to myself, Olive, you must always keep an eye out for Frankie! I made certain that you had each other. Olive was at her best during the visit.

Grammy and Poppy joined us as well. I once again put up my old camera and photographed everyone holding you. We framed all of the photos and hung them around the house. I frame images on your father's birthday, and we have a lovely collection of pictures and moments in all sizes all throughout our house. Something I always admired in the homes I visited as a child. And now we have that as well. Even though I'd only owned Olive for about a year and a half, I'd forgotten how everything worked, but it all came back to me. It's strange how your mind just goes blank, but the training wheels of fear had gone off, and I felt confident that everything would be fine this time. Your temperature, as well as vision and hearing examinations. I knew you'd be heavy enough. You were such a sweet little baby. You never cried or grumbled. Until it came time for dinner. And then you'd turn beet red in less than two seconds and find your war cry! You went from 0 to 60, and for the girl who was so happy and lovely, you wanted that food RIGHT NOW!!!!!!!!!!!!!!!!!!!!!!

And then you'd burp your way back to lovely, sweet Frankie. Which is what I spend my life listening for, with my ear to your chest, and you were fantastic at it, which was a huge comfort for both of us. There was never any conflict. You ate well, slept well, and smiled a lot. Even when you got a cold, you were always polite about it.

And as you grew bigger and bigger, you gained weight, right on schedule. I'd watch your blue eyes becoming bluer and your hair turn blonder. You were smitten by the bath. You were ecstatic to start eating solid foods, as if you had been waiting for it since day one. (You inherited your father's passion for food!)

But not your smile. Frankie, your grin is worth a million dollars. You glow like a Christmas tree and feel it all the way to the core of your existence. You are overjoyed. Happy. And a clinger in stage five. If I leave the room, you start crying. Or knock you down. Or pass you on to someone else. We call you rabbit legs because passing you is like passing a bunny who does not want to be handled. And when you're hurt, you thrust your arms forward, intertwining them with mine and clutching me until you calm down. It's fantastic. I like being of assistance to you.

I'm always trying different meals, and spaghetti with tomatoes is your ultimate favourite, and you can eat so much it worries me. I consider all of the tastes to offer to you, but I don't expect you to know every colour, animal, or number. You enjoy laughing and giggling with me. We both see the same thing, like you putting sand in your cracker bag and thinking it's the greatest thing ever. In that instant, we both do. We understand each other, and it's more about our sense of humour. At this stage, I'd rather have jokes than point out in a book, "This duck is yellow," even though you've discovered books and read them. I just know you'll catch up quickly, and I'm not worried about it because you'll have years in school and are more of a jock at this time anyhow.

I am certain you are a drummer. You even grip your sticks correctly and will perfectly adjust them if they slip. You have rhythm in both arms and put your entire self into it. It's incredible. (I've already registered you for music lessons. You begin in the fall.)

I'm sure you'll outgrow the need to be on my hip or in my arms soon. I can already feel it. You stroll and run around, doing things and going places. You will begin to gain independence, and all I can do is support and encourage you. This has all happened at the speed of light.

And I don't want you to grow too quickly, but I will shortly add another notch to the height chart I've been making for you and Olive on a wood beam on the wall (the kind I can take and retain if I need to—that's why I did it there). You'll start talking and telling me about yourself, rather than merely projecting that you enjoy smiling as much as I do. You're fantastic at doing your own thing, but I'm constantly nearby.

Just don't stop depending on me. That is why I am here. Your sister and you. To be present at every stage of the way. I daydream about the future. And my fantasies are consistent. They are you and your sister, and they make you feel as if you can always rely on me. For big and small things, as well as everything in between. I fear the days when you slam a door in my face (I'm not an idiot; I know what it's like to have two teenage girls), but I can manage it.

I was made for this. Indeed, I am looking forward to that. I shall always strive to choose the high road in life. Teach you to be thankful, courteous, and modest. It means the world to me. But you are also my teacher. And thus far, you've shown me that unconditional love is completely safe. My heart expanded the day you were born, and it continues to expand every time I see your grin.

To say I adore you is an understatement of the highest order. It will be my pride and joy to demonstrate what I will do for the rest of my life. As I sing to you to the tune of "Rubber Duckie"... "Little Frankie, I really like you."

CHAPTER 20

OUTWARD BOUND

Nan entered my office one afternoon in 1998 and said, "Oh my God, they're making Charlie's Angels at Sony!" We'll have to pitch ourselves." I was in the middle of stuffing cheap food into my face when she gave me indigestion. I was so wound up on our previous film, Never Been Kissed, because vanity deals were falling like flies, and if your film didn't work, you were done as a production business.

Taking on a massive action film appeared to be enough to get me to stop chewing long enough to say, "OK, tell me everything you know." She stated that the studio wanted to create the film but that the big idea was largely what they were working from and that they were seeking for someone to come in and own it and truly bring it to life!

Then she began talking about how she used to play Charlie's Angels with her buddies when she was younger. They'd all dress up as different angels and go solve crimes. Nan appears to be an original cast member, and I can imagine her well. And eventually, we went in and pitched the film and the world we wanted to build, as well as the tone and everything else. And, surprise, surprise, they invited us two ladies.

Then we wanted to hire a first-time director, get a script written with a brilliant writer and create three characters out of nowhere, convince everyone it would be great and to trust us, help in the hiring of all the team of costumes, makeup, and production design to set the look of the world, cast Cameron, find our third angel, Lovely Lucy, call a pay phone to find Bill Murray at a cryptic location and set a time after flying to New York to stalk him in person just to get him to talk on the phone, wrangle the brilliant Crispin Glover and convince the studio to cast an indie darling as the villain, try to combat all the negativity about how much this movie was going to suck from everyone including early press and Internet whispers by writing in the first scene of the film that we know we are making another movie out of an old television show and we are not taking ourselves so seriously so neither should you, keep convincing the studio we would not lose their $100 million investment, crusade for the angels not to use guns but use their brains and hand-to-hand combat instead, train for kung fu, and shoot a five-month-long action film. Then, once it's completed, you begin working with the marketing and PR departments to find out how you're going to sell this movie! From trailers and ads to posters and an international press tour, everything has been done.

Another option is to create a large number of magazine covers. So when Marie Claire recommended that the three angels go to Outward Bound since it would make a terrific story to promote the film, we all agreed. But then I moved to Boulder, Utah. We had just handed our first cut of the picture to the studio and were getting a lot of feedback.

It was three months until the film's release, and it was crunch time. We'd already been working on it for about a year, and I was exhausted and stressed. Instead of being a mature and rational person and reminding myself that I was fortunate to work with all of these amazing people and that it was all just a movie, I was wondering if all of my hard work to build a company would crash and burn in a very public and irreversible way. And this company had become both professionally and personally significant to me. I wanted to be at home, solving problems, and nowhere else.

These were my thoughts as we drove in a van to meet our "instructor," who wore a massive hat with the word "BOSS " inscribed on it. I was standing there as he told us that we'd be transported further out to a deserted area, dropped there, and collected up in three days. We planned to hike forty miles. We wouldn't have food, sleeping bags, or anything else. We only had the backpacks on our backs. Whhhhhh Aaaaaaaaaaa Tt???? What is going on? What am I doing? How did I get myself into this mess?

As we drove further, I observed that my companion angels were nowhere to be found. My entire vibe sucked, and as I stewed in the rear, I realised they had mutinied to avoid my toxic energy. Fuck. Cameron, Lucy, and I were often three content peas in a pod. We adored one another. We studied martial arts together. We all laughed together. They pushed and inspired one another. We spent weekends in Vegas together. They braided each other's hair. And yet, here I was, shunned because of my lousy attitude. "How did I get myself into this?" I kept thinking. Alternatively, "Do I want to sell a movie so badly that I'm willing to starve and freeze out in the wilderness for it?" There was no reaction. They weren't having any fun. They were there to have fun. Fuck fuck fuck fuck. The van continued going further out into the countryside, where no one could hear you and no one cared.

We started hiking the first night, and I just kept mumbling trash under my breath as I trailed everyone. Half because I just wanted to be alone, and half because my short legs couldn't keep up with me. I was the least athletic of the three of us. I could pretend and practice to be a badass, but there was no faking it out here. I was irritated because things had become far too real for me. The guide began by explaining how we would learn to create fire, survive, and obtain food in these conditions. He began by approaching a shrub and taking a clump of white straw off it, declaring, "This is peelu." It's a tree that's used in toothpaste and gum, but you can chew on it for hours and extract water and saliva out of it. It's pretty nice. Peelu is your pal. Make a mental note to look for some along our way." Go screw yourself.

That night, we walked for around five kilometres. The landscape resembled desiccated trees with orange and brown rocks. It looked like one of those places you fly over in a plane and think, wow, there's nothing but earth here, and if you zoomed thousands of miles down, you'd see us moving through it like tiny ants.

When it got dark, they led us over to a flat rock approximately fifteen by fifteen feet in size and stated, "You can all sleep here tonight." I asked Mr. Boss Hat, "Are you out of your fucking mind?" "You'll want to huddle together because body heat is all you have tonight," he continued. So the person in the middle will get the most heat, but I'd rotate all night if possible."

I was planning to murder someone. I was aware that my loving companions believed I should go suck an egg right now, and that no one wanted to spoon with me.

Instead, Lucy raised her hand like a good student and asked, "They told me that sleeping in the leaves is good too?" And, without taking too much delight in her attending our orientation, he remarked, "That's right. You may construct a pile of leaves to make it softer, and you can even use the leaves as a blanket."

Why wouldn't everyone do that, I reasoned? Why are you suggesting this damned rock, you idiot?

Everyone said good night and left, leaving us to our own devices to defecate in nature, brush teeth, enjoy the scenery, and so on. I just sat on the rock, enraged. From the corner of my eye, I noticed Lucy constructing her leaf bed, and I merely lay down on the rock, telling myself it was just temporary. I decided to join her there when she fell asleep and wasn't bothered by the fact that I was enveloping her from behind. As upset as the girls were at me, I think it was dawning on them that this was not going to be easy, and stuff just got real again. Nighty-night.

No chance. Lucy stood up from her leaves, shivering and chilled. "I need some heat!" Cameron motioned for her to come over, and the three of us settled into our three-way spoon positions. There was no time to sleep, not even a minute. We just rotated like three human skewers on a hibachi all night—the only one who wasn't dying was the one in the middle, and when your time was up, your time was over.

We barely said anything. We simply recognized what had to be done and executed it. We were thrilled for some warmth when the sun came up, and we cooked ourselves on that rock for at least a half hour. I heard crunching footsteps, followed by the boss and his cronies. "Good morning, everyone!" "Who's up for a twenty-mile walk?" My rage erupted all over again. We walked because we were tired and out of it. Again, I was either bringing up the back or pulling it down. In any case, I was back to muttering nonsense under my breath.

I was also quite hungry. I hadn't eaten much the day before while travelling, so it felt like two days without food, and it was just another thing to tip the balances of sanity versus lunacy. I was unbalanced and insane. All day I hiked, hiked, hiked, stopping for "life-saving tips" that I completely ignored. "I'd rather die out here," my inner monologue murmured, or "Kill me now and do me a favour." And if I ever got lost in the forest again, I'd definitely die, so there! Take it away, boss.

We had to start wearing carabiners. We were tied to the guides for safety as we dropped enormous stones and rocks into small streams and rivers. As we waded through the neck-high rivers, we'd hoist our little backpacks over our heads, and sometimes the backpack would come out dry, sometimes not. But now we were genuinely in the soil. If our hike the night before was a level one or two, this was a level nine or ten. We were truly a part of Mother Nature, slithering through her veins like blood.

We arrived at a large mountainside and began clipping back on to our separate folks, men who could give us slack and help us down if we fell because we were attached to them in case of emergency. I didn't even know what my guy's name was, although I'm typically the group leader. I am an extremely social person who typically draws people together. In fact, my girlfriends recognized me as the producer who made things happen and was there to smooth things over when necessary. We all did, we were a team, but I was used to being in a position of authority. I was now just dead weight, a carcass being lowered down a chasm.

Everyone made their way down. Lucy executed it beautifully, earning much applause and whoops from the audience, who exclaimed, "Great job, Lucy, you're like a spider!" and laughed. "OK, now it's your turn, Cameron!" they cried. She made her way down like the girl we all know and love, a born athlete from Long Beach, California. Cool, witty, and competent. Everyone burst out laughing.

Then a halfhearted person came to me. "OK, now it's your turn"—no name, just a "c'mon, let's get this over with and get the unfun one down the rock." That is exactly what I did. My foot slipped and I dropped ten feet, and then I snapped with a violent jerk as my tether caught, and I was simply swinging in midair, back and forth like a foolish metronome in unattractive khakis.

"FFFFFFFFFUUUUUUUUUUUUUUUUCCCCCCCCCKKKKKKKK KKKKK!" I screamed, and the bat flew away. I just cried and yelled as the guy lowered me down the mountain in midair, one awkward foot at a time. My knees buckled by the time my feeble feet hit the ground, and I lay there like a hog-tied loser, all tangled up in my ropes and lines.

A few humble and vulnerable hours later, I stood back and observed as the entire group bonded. Lucy caught a fish with her bare hands in the river (which she subsequently puked out of her intestines), and everyone cooked and ate it, slapping her back as they did so. "How great was this!" Cameron exclaimed. (She later contracted the parasite giardia.) Wow. Everyone admired them for their team spirit and positive outlook.

What was the matter with me? Why was I at the end of my tether in every way? I was wailing in the bushes alone, fiercely eating peelu because no one would officially speak to me. What was going on in my life? Was this my midlife crisis? I was twenty-five. Maybe this was it when you start work at basically one and enjoy life in the fast lane.

I was under a lot of stress and couldn't filter it in a healthy way. I'd just revert to being a small kid who had never been taught how to manage situations. But in real life, I don't boo-hoo. When something goes wrong, I pick up the pieces.

"Well, once again, you'll have to figure things out for yourself," I heard myself remark. You've come to the bushes for a reason, and you require an epiphany. And initially, you must begin eating, licking your wounds, and gradually work your way back into everyone's good graces."

I was spiralling inward rather than forth, and I needed to correct this. So I stood up, walked over to the nature-loving circle, and joined in. I sat a few feet away, like if a dog had done something extremely bad and was slowly worming its way back in. That's me. The filthy tiny pup.

That night, I'd softened the females enough to re-enter the spoon, and we rotated all night. We tried the leaves this time, and they were a little better, but it was all about the human burrito. It's as simple as that. We went several miles the next day and arrived at a magnificent river. They said we could wash in there later, but first we had to learn how to build fire!

They led us to a cave to set up a day tent where the wind would be gentler. They had us take our sticks and twine and fashion a bow-and-arrow-style contraption to create the friction that would spark the fire. Then they discussed the kindling—finding something light, wispy, and flammable and making a little bird's nest out of it. You could also rub two rocks together until a spark appears over your kindling and start your fire that way.

Lucy chose the two-rocks method, but Cameron chose the bow-friction method. I, too, selected the latter. They both had fire within thirty minutes and were applauded for it. In terms of encouragement from the guides, I had worked my way back into the group during the previous twelve hours, earning a token "keep going, you can do it" salute. I still had no fire three agonising hours later. My scraped palm was bleeding, and I was silently wiping away the last of my tears from the day before. "Motherfucker, I will never get this, fuck!" I continued telling myself silently.

I continued rubbing, pushing, and tugging. I looked like a crazed monkey, jerking my arm back and forth in an attempt to start a fire. I was not going to give up. I was tempted to simply turn around and tell everyone, "You know what, I tried, and I know you're all disappointed, but I just couldn't do it, so let's just chalk it up to me being the one who dies out in the wilderness." I could do a lot of other things in life, but this was not one of them. I felt ill and guilty as I swallowed my defeat and my arm began to slow. I was leaving. My arm had practically come to a halt at this point, with just a few dejected rubs to appear to be doing it rather than actually doing it.

My inner voice suddenly came to life, and it sounded nothing like the one that had been practising my justifications for the past few hours. I heard it, the volume quickly ratcheting up like a dial: NO! You are not going to give up! You never, ever give up! It makes no difference what shit you get yourself into. YOU NEVER GIVE UP!!!! With each phrase of militant encouragement, I began to work my arm a bit faster. I was my own drill sergeant, telling myself, "Get up, you fucking loser, and don't be such a loser!" I went faster, faster, faster, causing much more significant friction than previously. It wasn't going to happen. Still? Why? How long will it take? My voice responded to me. It will require everything! Nothing is easy. Earn it, for God's sake! As a result, I did. I threw everything I had into it, and the entire world faded away, leaving only the silence of my mind, which had been so noisy with negativity the previous few days. Now everything was clear, and I could concentrate. I don't care if your hand falls off; you're going to start a fire!

I continued at a frantic, muscular out-of-body pace. And then I heard more voices wash in like waves on the beach: You're doing it! You are succeeding! I opened my eyes, and there it was! Smoke!!!!!!!! I couldn't stop myself. On some insane autopilot, I kept flinging my arm back and forth, staring around with wild eyes. The guys dashed over and exclaimed, "OK, now pull back and start blowing on it!" "If you keep going, it will go out," he continued, looking at me, still pressing and pulling. You must slow down and start the kindling before the smoke turns to flame." I was terrified of stopping, as if everything might fall apart.

But I did it. I came to a slow halt and began blowing. "Slower, less wind, you don't want to blow it out," the guy added. Slow," I said into my small smoking bird's nest, and then it occurred. It exploded into a little flame right in front of my eyes. I looked up, my eyes watery and regretful, so excited. And my girlfriends stared at me proudly. They were aware of what I was going through and simply wanted to see me succeed. Friends do things like that.

Later that night, the boys told us they had a surprise for us. And they rolled out three sleeping bags that they had to have up their asses because they appeared out of nowhere. On second thought, there was a new guy in our group that day. Perhaps he brought them.

But I was overjoyed, and I couldn't have enjoyed it as much if I hadn't been through what I had. It's as simple as that. Everything must be removed. It has in my life as well. When I was thirteen, everything vanished, and I lost my job, my credibility, and my independence, and I had to rebuild everything. But, unlike the fire, I did not give up. I didn't do it gracefully, but I fought my way into something better and more enlightened. I'll have many more rounds in life. But this was a significant one. My lesson here was to never give up. You hold yourself responsible. You continue to be appreciative. You cling to your pals tightly.

I was both exhausted and content. The other girls and I split up since we were all excited to explore this place on our own for one night after being velcroed together for the previous two. I dozed off. A deep and restful slumber among the moon and stars. I slept in Mother Nature's embrace, despite being in my nice Eddie Bauer sleeping bag. When I awoke, the three of us reunited, finally alone, and took a lengthy dip in the river. We stripped naked and took a naked birdbath in the middle of nowhere. It was a special occasion, and we were all aware of it. Life is pictured in your mind. When we rejoined the group, we hiked for a few kilometres before returning to the location where we would be picked up in the van. It was shocking how different I felt than when it dropped me off. But now I'm altered and refreshed. I got in the vehicle and drove to my usual seat in the back, this time by choice rather than rejection. I took a look out the window. I heard the voice in my head speak again, and this time the tone was different, calm and gentle. "You never give up, and you wonder how you got here," it said. Did you put yourself in that position? Can you find a way out? That was the end of your lesson. Don't forget about that."

I told myself I wouldn't. I swear I won't. And I didn't do it. I returned home, and the picture was a huge success. And once again, I was relieved. But, more importantly, I had matured a little more. I did it just when I needed to.

CHAPTER 21

AFRICA

I was having breakfast alone in a coffee cafe one day in 2004. We were making the picture Fever Pitch at the time, and it was a very happy period. The Red Sox were winning and on their way to making history. When I was unmarried and reading the New York Times, I came upon an article. It wrote, "Children line up to get into the classroom," and it was accompanied by a picture showing hundreds of youngsters sitting on the floor in orderly rows, facing toward the front of the class. These kids had this gorgeous and eager look in their eyes. It was diametrically opposed to the look I saw in the classroom in my personal experience. These kids fought tooth and nail to get in. And, when I read further, it had to do with the World Food Program giving meals. My heart was broken.

At that moment, I couldn't have felt more humbled, and something took over. I was overcome by empathy and curiosity. I wished I could be transferred there right then and there so I could better understand the universe of this tiny school. Something inside of me was stirred to the point where I went home and picked up the phone, only to discover I didn't know who to contact.

So I started calling people I used to work with. I was then assigned to the United Nations. When I first approached them, I presented myself as a volunteer who wanted to learn. Their concern was not to take on some celebrity looking for a photo op, which I very appreciated. I explained that I was also allergic to it, and that this was not it. This was me, a little human attempting to learn how their programs worked. They praised me for my interest and promised to contact me later. I got the call a year later.

It came from Marie Claire magazine. They had heard that I was interested in visiting Africa and had contacted the UN. They would help me travel there if I wrote an article about my journey. They served as both my connection and my finances. I was quite excited since I had an assignment. I was supposed to fly to Kenya and meet a UN relief worker at the airport. Ben was his name. He was British and exuded the impression of "I despise celebrities." Oh, no. "Listen, Florence Nightingale, don't try to make it seem like you care because this is a full-time job, not a swoop-in-and-snap-a-picture-and-leave situation," he might as well have said. It was the same as when I called. I once again admired this.

We began by visiting Kibera, which they referred to as a slum and was one of the most densely populated neighbourhoods in Africa, much alone Nairobi. We travelled in UN vehicles with the two UN initials painted on the sides. Ben explained that this was done to let people know who we were since the UN was viewed as a friend, not a foe. The UN had no agenda and was usually a symbol of assistance since if you were perceived as a threat in these places, you may be killed. Simply put, these were extremely unsafe environments, and my first wave of "what am I doing here?" washed over me. Trash was piled so high that it reached the height of a two-story structure. There was filthy water everywhere. People lived and worked in tiny little stores that were 10 by ten feet with a cot on the floor. There was an entire world inside these places, and many people merely departed to work elsewhere. As bad as the infrastructure was, it was quite insular. I'd never seen anything like it.

When we arrived at the school, the few individuals in charge came out to greet us. We all exchanged handshakes and introduced ourselves. But then a flurry of bright colours swept over my view, and the youngsters began pouring out of the small structure to form a line. They were preparing to perform a greeting ceremony that had obviously been scripted. The outer world and sadness faded away, and the joy of these children transformed my life forever. It was a Technicolor awakening. We spent the entire day with the children. They took me into the classroom I had fantasised about for the previous year after their dancing and singing. It was dark since the only light came in through fractures and a few cut-open places in the walls. The flags and miniature quilts produced by the teachers and hung on the walls were both educational and poetic. This room felt welcoming, and I knew I was in the proper place.

I sat in on a lesson and observed these students practising their English and maths skills. I asked each of the children what they wanted to be when they grew up. One student raised her hand. "A pilot." "Really," I said, astounded by her response. And I answered, "You can take everyone to see the whole world." The next person to speak raised his hand. "A doctor." "Wonderful," I remarked, "you can take care of everybody," and they chuckled. Not a giddy laugh, but a hopeful one. Another child raised his or her hand. "A scientist." "Well," I explained, "you will solve all the problems." Another chuckle.

It astounded me that they were all realistic and ambitious jobs. There were no plans to become an artist, a mother, or a singer. They wanted to make a difference in the world. My heart moved and expanded once more. They took me to the smallest closet, which was the kitchen, at the end of the day: a wood-burning improvised stove on the ground with a large tin pot on it. The pot contained porridge as well as oil, and the oil was rich in nutrients and vitamins. The World Food Program stepped in to help. Ben stated that the youngsters each received one or two cups, one in the morning and one at lunch. It was a red plastic cup with a handle. The kids would sometimes preserve some of their meals to go home and share with their families.

However, without this initiative, many children would have struggled to acquire any food at all. It was one of the reasons they came to school in the first place. To receive an education while also being nourished. I pretended to be taking it all in because I didn't want to cry. I was afraid Ben would kill me because I was a weak starlet who couldn't handle the hard realities of these circumstances. I just kept writing things down in my notebook and making notes, remaining stoic. I used a journalistic approach. After all, I had stated to the UN that I was here to study. And I would do exactly that.

I couldn't sleep once we got home that night due to jet lag and everything I had witnessed that day. When morning arrived, I was excited to return to Kibera and learn more. We were now joined by Lionello, a man from the UN headquarters who lived in Geneva and ran the offices. We'd be attending a different school that day. This school was mainly concerned with female issues. Rape and genital mutilation were major issues in this region.

I took out my notes once more and asked questions, but I was dying on the inside. I was once again in over my head. I wanted to confront kids at school, and I was learning about the food they fought to consume and the circumstances in which they lived. This was more about survival, and schooling was a huge luxury. I was nearly catatonic. But when I noticed Ben looking at me for a reaction, I kept my cool. I wasn't going to give him the joy of seeing me break like a b*tch. I was surrounded by people who dealt with this on a daily basis; they were the heroes, and all I wanted to do was be quiet, courteous, and keep up.

We walked past the school, and the students sang us another greeting song. It was stunning. I was so shaken when they started that I wondered what I thought I could ever do here. How can I assist? When these youngsters' voices overcame the self-doubting ones in my thoughts, I felt completely out of my league and completely inadequate. Their music and delight completely cleared the slate, and I persuaded myself that it was all about them. If the World Bank is unable to solve poverty issues, and I am unable to safeguard each and every one of them as I would like, because no one can, I can only strive to assist specific schools. I could try to assist these establishments one at a time. Perhaps just start with one.

Ben stated that it was not that straightforward, and that all donations go into a blanket surplus for all schools or emergency situations. In most crisis situations around the world, the UN and the World Food Programme are among the first to arrive on the scene. I felt I'd found the proper place with the WFP; the question was, what role did I play in all of this?

I spent the rest of the week there visiting several schools in various places. We eventually ventured far outside of the city, into rural areas. We drove past a vast vista that is nothing more than an imprinted crater in the earth as far as the eye can see, and I sat on the side of the road, amazed. The schools outside of town represented a complete change in terrain and facility. Many of these schools were live-in boarding schools with their own land. They had a quieter and calmer feeling, despite the fact that it was arid or not as welcoming as you would like. Space. The threats were not ten feet away. They were no different in terms of what they needed, and they relied on school meal programs and contributions to stay afloat.

Following that, I was escorted around a couple Masai Mara tribe settlements. This was when I saw a portion of Africa that seemed both grandiose and familiar. They wore bright red plaid that was wrapped around them. They wore huge wooden hoop earrings on their lobes, black and white tribal marks on their skin, and beaded necklaces up to their chins. It was stunning and wonderful.

I was taken there to learn about the origins of many traditions and to gain a better understanding of how these people lived. They resided in huts built by the women. Every night, the men went to a different one. The youths were sent out into the Mara on warrior missions to mature into men. And the girls had a road laid out for them a long time ago. Again, this was a centuries-old practice that should not be questioned, especially not by me. But I could see how the girls who could go to school were experiencing a different way of life. Everything appeared so far away in nature. Despite this, the girls arrived from there. As a result, it was really useful in informing me.

Lionello suggested we'd stop somewhere else on the way home. It served as a children's hospice. This specific small girl began walking by my side as soon as we pulled over and got out of the car. I smiled at her, and we continued to stare at each other, a cute cat-and-mouse game of glances. We entered the structure, which was a small hospital with concrete walls rather than mud or wood. It was modest and quaint, yet it had a lovely atmosphere. It was still in a dangerous neighbourhood, but it felt safe, and I was relieved that the kids had a safe place to stay until I understood why they were there. All of the kids had different illnesses, and I got to know them and their stories.

The small girl who had been following me had moved in next to me. I kept an eye on her. I had spent my entire life with grownups, and without brothers or relatives, I just did not have a relationship with small children. In fact, I was aware that they might detect my terror. Then I became unappealing since I didn't know how to relate to them. Kids are also instinctive, and I could tell they could always detect my incapacity to participate.

So I was being polite with this lovely little kid till I dared to ask her name. "Edith," they said, because she could only communicate in Swahili. However, not having to use words most likely aided us. Within a few minutes, she had my hands in hers. Even when I tried my hardest with children, they didn't appreciate it. I was basically a failure at being what kids wanted or needed, and by my thirties, I had given up trying. I basically ignored myself and hung around with the adults. But by wanting to be with me, Edith was paying me the highest compliment of my life. I was not only humbled and honoured in ways I had never known before, but I was also glad for her unspoken relationship.

I can honestly say that as the day progressed, I fell in love. Her gentle charm and care awoke something inside me that had been dormant since I was a child, not realising what a child is. We were like two peas in a pod, each providing what the other required. I inquired about Lionello's presence. "She has AIDS," he explained. "Oh." I agreed by nodding. And I gripped her hand even tighter.

I was trembling when it was time for us to pack things and depart. I didn't want to let go of Edith. Unwrapping my fingers from hers was a betrayal of the bond we had created on that fateful day. I kissed her goodbye and held her repeatedly. We got in the car, and I waved to her as we drove away until she was no longer visible. I turned around and lost it when I looked out the windshield. I was overcome with emotion. Hopeless. Hopeful. Changed. Clear. Convicted. I looked at Lionello. "I want to sponsor her." He questioned what I meant, and I replied, "I'm not sure, but I need you to help me." I need your assistance in establishing a trust for her and directing the funds to her. "Are you capable of doing that?"

After weeks of hearing how difficult it is to raise cash to make an individual difference and how the UN is saving lives with fifty cents a day, I realised there was a huge gap between miracles happening and there still being so much to accomplish. Starting with her was a means for me to figure out how to give money in a constructive, personal, and meaningful way. I'd get to the more serious economic issues once I'd understood more. "We will get it done," Lionello assured, and I breathed for the first time since we left that children's hospital. I glanced out the window, taking in a place I had no idea I'd be visiting a year ago.

I felt like I really experienced distinct landscapes by the conclusion of my journey. For hours and hours, we took propeller planes and extended rides through the terrain. Marie Claire even sent me to a safari lodge for a night to express her gratitude for publishing this piece. When we returned to Nairobi, the bustling metropolis felt like a bizarre utopia. Nonetheless, there was disagreement. I was both bewildered and awake. As I was leaving in the morning, our little crew agreed to go out for a drink that night.

We discussed the previous ten days and exchanged personal information; we were getting to know each other better. It was good to unwind for a while. That's what surprised me. These UN employees were very amusing. They didn't want to wallow all the time. They probably wouldn't survive if they did. They were matter-of-fact about the challenges because they were in it, doing what they could to solve it, rather than cowering in fear at its enormity. They appeared to be superheroes, but they were pulling off their masks, drinking, and demonstrating that they couldn't be more human. And entertaining humans at that.

Ben seemed different the next morning when he drove me to the airport. Less judgemental and more laid-back. But as he led me to the check-in counter, he continued, "You know when you got here—" I cut him off: "I know. You despised me." "No," he responded, smiling and shaking his head. "I just wanted to know if you were full of shit, and it appears that you aren't." Phew. Ben was providing his unique stamp of approval. He even said, "Come back," out of nowhere. I knew there was a part of him that was thinking, "Because I bet you won't," and I smiled at him immediately. "I will," I responded, adding, "Watch me, fucker!" And with that, we silently dared each other, and I walked away to catch my flight. I wrote my article all the way home because I had plenty of time and wanted to write it as soon as possible after the experience.

When I visited a food shop after a few days of being home, I was amazed at how much abundance we have. I became really unhappy, guilty, and disoriented. I felt as if I couldn't look at anything the same way again. Despite this, I had barely scratched the surface. What was I thinking? I knew this was my life out here, but there was something else I couldn't turn off.

After a few weeks of wandering around, I took the initiative and phoned the UN again—"I'd like to go back, please"—and a few months later, I was flying back. As I strolled through the airport, I noticed my greeter. Instead of being shy, I approached Ben and asked, "Did ya miss me?" because we didn't need to debate the fact that I had accepted his silent bet and was returning. And for a couple weeks this time!

"Let's do this," I thought, and we went straight into a refugee camp. And, as nervous as I was, I felt like the training wheels had come off. There was no one paying for this trip, and it was time to delve even further into the world I had grown to care about.

The refugee camp was enormous. Our bunks were in a secure fenced-in UN area, with tiny concrete constructions about ten by ten feet in size, each with a single cot and a small wooden table and lamp. That was it, and yet it seemed incredibly welcoming. Again, it is a fantastic privilege in comparison to how some people live. And you are perfectly aware of any gifts you receive. We were served Ethiopian food and a beer for dinner. Tusker lager. And we drank one under a tree with bugs falling from it. They'd come crashing down on your skull. The bugs were so big that you'd jump out of your folding chair and run at least ten feet, and everyone would mock you for being so afraid. But, even though they insisted they were safe, these bugs were the size of small bats, and I couldn't help but freak out.

That was a night I'll never forget. It was a chance to unwind while being assaulted by enormous showering insects.

We began the following day. I was on another school tour because I wanted to improve my dedication. I was very interested in schools, and they were a deliberate target. I felt like I might be useful there. It was odd that I didn't prioritise school in my own life, but was moved by how these youngsters fought to be here. I'd go to each one and find out what they actually needed. They lacked something. And what was causing them to thrive.

Some children were forced to go too far, which made it unsafe or difficult. Villages without water were a big challenge. Schools with a boarding component were more attractive in more remote areas, but sanitation was a concern in more populated towns.

Again, it can become extremely daunting very quickly, but I spent three weeks studying what needed to be done. The World Food Program introduced me to Paul Tergat, an Olympic athlete who benefited from the school feeding program. He was able to train and run because of the food, and he understood what it would take to get himself to a situation where he could have opportunity because of the education. He took me to his old school, where he and I planted a tree. It was a very joyful school with a small plot of land, and the kids were so lively and entertaining. We went to his old house in the neighbourhood, where I met his family.

It was incredible to be working with someone who was living proof of what was possible, and he had important things to say about how everything worked. We then travelled to several parts of Kenya. And I fell madly in love with Kiltamany. Building a borehole here would revolutionise the entire area, bringing water to a spot where residents had to go at least five miles a day to fill a little pitcher. And there was a school and a lot of kids, and it looked like a great place to start. The people were extremely friendly and helpful. There was a neighbourhood. And that affected me and left an indelible mark on me.

When I was going to leave this time, I had a serious conversation with Ben and Lionello about what we could accomplish first. What it would cost, and what the priorities were. First, there was money to keep schools in the districts running for a year. Then it was assisting in the construction of these advanced boreholes, which delivered water to areas in need. Then there was the question of whether I should create my own school and, if so, where.

I'd travelled to so many places by this point—where did I sense a connection to creating a foundation that could be kept and monitored? It was a lot to take in, and I didn't want to just donate money and not know where it went, but I also recognized how much money was required. How could I be the most efficient?

When I returned to America, I went to the United Nations in New York and received my full ambassadorship. I collaborated with a woman named Bettina, and we devised strategies for raising awareness about the initiative. It was the best day of my life when I received my UN passport. I was very proud and delighted to be a part of something so meaningful and helpful. So I went out touring regions on behalf of the World Food Program, trying to spread the word. I wanted to fulfil my role by not just donating my own money but also getting others interested. But my groundwork was my favourite. When I was genuinely there and no one knew where I was, I was at my best. I decided to create my school and chose Isiolo as the site. I began collecting blueprints and plans. I couldn't contain my excitement. Things were actually occurring, and I was overjoyed.

When I started seeing my husband, Will, who was just my boyfriend at the time, around two years later, I got a call saying the school was ready to be viewed. It wasn't entirely operational yet, but it was poised to make the final decisions. I'd never brought anyone with me on these outings. They were quite individual for me, and I had yet to share any of this with anyone. But I took a chance and asked Will if he wanted to go see it with me. He responded unequivocally yes, and off we went to Africa. I had something to show this time, and I was quite excited to welcome him into my world.

We arrived at the school site after many days and hours of travel. There were already kids present. I entertained all of the children while we served lunch. They led me over to a small painted sign that read "The Barrymore Learning Academy" in hand-painted lettering, and everything felt so genuine and joyful at the time that I could have burst.

Will then brought out his camera and photographed me with the kids under the placard. Click. And I knew right then and there that my concerns about my energy and how children interpreted it were over. I felt healed of something that had always been painful as a result of my learning what they need. A kid who didn't know how to interact with other kids. But not any longer. I was free to love. My heart was the most open it had ever been in my life.

I went to see Edith before we departed. She had grown so nicely. She was taller and in better health. I rushed up to her and introduced her to Will. We'd all met in a park, where her trust-funded caretaker had taken her. I spent the afternoon threading my fingers through hers and holding her hand. I was overjoyed to see her again. I was overjoyed to see how content she was. Even so, she maintained her cool. But her smile remained the same. I'm grateful she selected me in this world. I consider myself fortunate. I can only try to repay the favour. And this time, when we said our goodbyes, I wasn't in tears because I knew she'd be fine. We hugged for five minutes nonstop.

Something had changed inside of me by the time I returned home from this vacation. I considered getting ready to have my own children. It was time to begin learning about and investing in what it meant to be a caring mother. I knew I was prepared. This decade altered my life. My entire life could have been different if I hadn't read the article in the diner that day. Or are we established on routes we must follow, with small bread crumbs beckoning us in? I'm not sure, but I now know a lot more than I did before.

And these are the teachings and values I intend to inculcate in my daughters. They'll have to figure out what's important to them, but I'm glad our house will be supportive of that. I now prepare a Hallmark card for the girls on Mother's Day to tell them what I did in their honour. I make donations, travel to drop off gifts, or we organise a volunteer day. It is always for children's charity. That is what interests me. That is what moves me. And, until my children are old enough to find out what their cause is, I will do it for them so that they may get a head start on everything.

This is quite important in my life. I hope I can motivate them. I will give it my all. And this is where I believe in the idea that children learn by example. My stupid dances will not teach them much. But, ideally, I can be of use in encouraging them to think beyond themselves. Africa served as a wake-up call for me. And I am grateful that the UN responded to my request.

CHAPTER 22

IN-LAW JACKPOT

During the spring, I entered my Upper East Side apartment for the first time. Will and I had only been together for a few months. It was my first visit to his parents' house, where he had grown up. I moved from room to room, taking everything in. The artwork shown on the walls. There are family photos everywhere, in frames and on the wall. There was a library in the room. A warm and well-appointed kitchen. But I was smitten by the remaining old-school cordless phone from the 1980s.

There was an evident sense of warmth. And all of the photos I kept looking at revealed a tale about this close-knit family. Will was at college with his parents the night before a school play. As children, he and his sister, Jill, played in a flower field. Will as a baby snoozing on the beach. On their honeymoon, grandparents. I took them all in, fitting them together like a puzzle to figure out what was going on in my boyfriend's life. Not only was it different from my own—sure, we both had a set of fancy grandparents—but this entire existence of "togetherness captured" was strange and, to be honest, terrifying.

My West Hollywood urchin began to kick in. "You don't belong here," my inner voice said, and the hardest part was trying to look at his parents. Arie and Coco Kopelman had been married for 39 years, and they had two children, William and Jill. They had a lovely life. Excellent schools for all generations. Extensive international travel. Arie used to be a "mad man" advertising at DDB, one of the major agencies in the 1960s. He was not only brilliant and creative, but he was also a brilliant businessman.

So one of his accounts, Chanel, with whom he had worked in advertising for fifteen years, contacted one day and said, "We want you to come run our company and become president here." They are a family-owned French enterprise, and they joked that where else would they find a man named Coco? It was almost too perfect. He worked there for twenty years, retired, and is still on the board.

Coco and Arie first met in college. She was a French girl living in Manhattan, attending Parsons School of Design, and had aced her baccalaureate exams due to her exceptional intelligence. Coco Franco, a smart, stylish twenty-year-old, met Arie Kopelman, and on their first date, he took her to the city's '21' Club. Things went so well that three months later, on her twenty-first birthday, he proposed to her at the '21' Club. (Arie's favourite number is twenty-one.)

So that's what I knew. This was all I knew when Will mentioned that his parents wanted to meet me for supper. I proposed the '21' Club as a fun idea, and they agreed. But I was terrified on the inside. Do they want me? Will they be sceptics? Were they cold individuals, despite their apartment's appearance? Would they glance at me with that "prove it" expression on their face? After all, I was dating their son.

This felt like the most important audition of my life. Despite the fact that Will and I had only been dating for a few months, the girl in me felt compelled to mature with him. I could tell this was different. I was a "this is who I am" kind of person. I'd spent my entire life digging in my heels with guys, and now I wasn't fighting for the same things. I could imagine myself spending my life with this man. Although it was new, the stakes felt tremendous.

So I rounded the bend from the hallway and heard their voices. Will was plainly hugging his mother, and I overheard Arie asking a question. All I remember is that I was looking down at the ground. My heart was racing. Most people dislike their partner's parents. This is a proven fact. There are movies about it, such as The In-Laws, that depict the challenges of the family meeting the new girlfriend and then everything goes insane.

I inhaled deeply. My eyes finally raised, and before I could glance at their expressions, Coco was stretching herself and hugging me. I noticed Arie looking over her shoulder with a big loving smile. I began to relax my tight body and transform into a thankful girl who no longer felt condemned. Perhaps I had judged myself? I was concerned about a possible preconception of the "actress girl" Will was bringing home, and as that intimidation faded, being my own person took over, and I was free to simply be myself, which is always the greatest way to be. However, it is extremely beneficial when others disarm you. Especially when they take you in their arms.

We went on a fantastic double date to the famous '21' Club. There were vintage model planes hanging from the ceiling and beer steins all around the bar in the dining area. To match the mood of the evening, the area had character and warmth. Arie ordered martinis while Coco had steak Diane.

We discussed our lives and got to know one other. Coco is clever and extremely intelligent. Sunday-New York Times crossword, graduate early, speak multiple languages, and know everything that is going on in the world cleverly. Did I mention her incredible sense of style? She was also training to be a ballerina, so she had grace and poise, but the best part is that she laughs hysterically at a joke. She appreciates people being themselves, and the entire family has a great sense of humour.

Arie and I shared a passion for hearts. I informed him that I was writing a book about them. He likes antique Americana paintings, and hearts are a large part of his collection. He is also interested in history and preservation. And, as luck would have it, he is on the board of a whaling museum, and I had just finished a film on whales and had read thousands of pages about them while stuck up in Alaska by myself for months on end, and I was so happy to share it with someone. Not everyone is interested in discussing the complexities of whales. But we did it.

It was a perfect evening, and that night I fell in love—not just with Will, but also with his parents. They were everything you could hope for: kind, worldly, and humorous. Their family unit's strong stability and plentiful love helped completely clear what I was feeling within that felt a little unfamiliar.

I was also thinking about my family. I wasn't a girl who had a crush on a boy. I was asking myself, "How will this all function?" and a lot of that is determined by the decisions you make. A child was the one thing I swore I would take seriously. As severe as a heart attack. It was the one thing I would never, ever mess up. If there was any doubt, I knew I would never have children.

I come from a model of what not to do, and I wouldn't even think about having children until I had a tangible antidote to my experience.

Will and I took off after an old-fashioned meeting of the parents. We spent a year travelling throughout the world. Travel provides an excellent response to the age-old question of "how will this function?" Nancy always compares love to The Amazing Race. She asks, "Do you want to be the couple that works well together or the couple that doesn't?" That is correct. I used to be late for everything, pack at the last minute, and make travelling to the airport a stressful experience, and Will finally said, "No more." He said it brought him too much anxiety.

So, for the first time, instead of saying my standard "this is who I am," I considered how it might sound. "No, I enjoy being a slob who gives everyone an ulcer on travel day, only to miss the flight and ruin the trip." That wasn't worth fighting for, so I agreed and began packing the night before.

We travelled from Austin to Africa. My favourite trip was to Hawaii. We rented a house, cooked, and went hiking. For the first time in my life, I slept soundly. We used to travel to New York to visit his folks. I met Jill, his sister, and her three children, Sadie, Ivy, and Fletcher—each one unique but all wonderful. They are fearless, and Jill encourages their independence like no one else.

Jill was like a light bulb went out. I couldn't believe my eyes or hearing when I first saw her. Jill may be described as a cross between Morticia Addams and Oscar Wilde, with a dash of Lucille Ball thrown in for good measure. She is brassy, daring, and astute. She's the woman at the table who has everyone wide-eyed but laughing uncontrollably at the things she says. And you enjoy it. But she is also wonderfully thoughtful, always has her thank-you cards ready, and is the type of person you want to spend the evening with. I fell in love once more.

Will and Jill were arranging a surprise 40th anniversary party for Arie and Coco in Idaho, where the family has spent every Christmas since Arie and Coco met. This was the big one, and it happened on December 26th, and I was simply watching in awe. Will and Jill read aloud a poem they composed for their parents in this little gathering of around forty people who have all known this family since the beginning. It was the finest and funniest thing you have ever heard.

The snow fell outside as we sat in this cosy tiny room with close friends and relatives. And I had a strange feeling as we drove home. When we got inside, I lit the candle for the night because I had brought a portable menorah. It was the seventh night of Chanukah, and I wanted to do something special to commemorate Will, who is Jewish. We lit the candle and expressed our gratitude for this unforgettable evening.

We were as warm in our hearts as the flame we held, and the quantity of love and goodness I had just witnessed made me dizzy. Will said he'd be right back, and I didn't pay attention to what he was doing. I just stood there staring at the raging flames. I was in a haste at the time. I turned around to see Will on his knee, holding a ring box.

Oh my goodness. I have no idea what we said at that moment, but I do know that we both fought to get here. And, despite the fact that our paths had plainly diverged, we had found our way to this love. And we knew we wanted to expand on that love. So I said yes, and three weeks later I discovered I was pregnant.

We, of course, informed Arie and Coco first. I was so delighted to have a child in this people's environment that I knew I was on the correct track to doing everything differently. This secure, indestructible family was adding a new member, and I was overjoyed. We all agreed that the wedding would take place in June, when I would be six months pregnant. I loved the thought of our child being able to attend!

And I phoned Arie as we were arranging the wedding. "Hello, Arie," I introduced myself. "Oh, Drew," he said, yelling for Coco to pick up the phone. When one of their children calls, they always do this. Coco, I imagined, picked up the cordless phone from the 1980s to join the call. "Hi, guys," I introduced myself. "We've been planning, and I had a question for you both." Of course, they replied. "Coco, did you want to walk down the aisle with Will so that we could all walk together?" And Arie, I was wondering whether you'd be willing to hand me away?" He took another. "Oh wow," he exclaimed. "Are you sure?" "Of course!" says one. There's no other way I can imagine it." We did because he said yes.

When the four of us were getting set to walk down the aisle together that day, I looked around. Sadie, Ivy, and Fletcher were flower girls and boys, Jill was about to read a section from The Velveteen Rabbit, and I noticed Coco. I could tell she was sincerely content. She was brushing away a tear as she kissed Will, and all I could think was that I had to constantly make her feel like he was pleased as well. I adore and esteem her tremendously. I hoped to be a mother in some way like Coco. She is my female role model. She grabbed Will's arm. As we proceeded down the aisle, Arie raised my veil and kissed my cheek as I approached the chuppah. Check! It's a little girl fantasy! My wish had been granted.

My husband gave a beautiful speech that night, and all of the Kopelmans' lifelong friends were present, which I thought was essential, as were all of my friends, who were my original family. Jill delivered the best speech ever, which had everyone howling, and, most importantly, Olive was present. Our unnamed daughter, who was going to become the apple of her grandparents' eyes.

Arie came to me after Olive was born and remarked, with his trademark whole-face smile, "There's nothing overrated about being a grandparent," and he means it. Olive and her cousins have the nicest grandparents imaginable. When Frankie, our second daughter, was born, he said the same thing. They were present for both births and held each girl for several hours after she was born.

And every time I saw them holding their granddaughters, all wrapped up, fresh and new after their lengthy voyage in my body, I thanked God for Will's parents. I adore them to pieces. For the first time, I am a member of a family. In life's lottery, I won the in-law jackpot. The colossal one.

CHAPTER 23

ALL-AGES PARTY

I never know how old somebody is. I have no idea whether someone is thirty or fifty. I'm not sure if you're twenty-three or thirty-three years old. And I have no experience with children. Babies I can now nail because I am a mom who has gone through three years of stages, so I can tell you how old your child is to the week in a split second.

But I don't know my age since one important lesson my mother taught me was that age didn't matter. As a result, I was taught not to pay attention. She would be vehement about someone being adult or immature, but it was never about a number. She stated that young individuals may be wise above their years, whilst elderly people may be childish.

She never asked someone their age and lied about her own. I had to sneak in once while she was showering and dig into her handbag like a robber and pull out her driver's licence to check the age. When I approached her, she said that it wasn't true since they had to fabricate a birth certificate for her because she was born in a displaced persons camp in Germany and hence had no legitimate birth certificate. As a result, the driver's licence was incorrect. Then I'd question her for her true birth date, and she'd just look at me with a sly smirk, as if I'd been duped again, and saunter out of the room, leaving me bewildered and unsure what to believe.

Was she telling the truth? And, if so, about what part was she lying? What is your age? What about the diploma? I'd start looking up German camp years in history, but without the Internet or encyclopaedias, I'd forget by the time I got there. When I started school, my schools were always hippy shambles with no proper library.

I suppose I could have asked someone, but a seven-year-old asking about a displaced persons camp looked unusual, and asking anyone felt risky. What was her name? What was her age? What was my age? I wasn't feeling seven. I felt my age. And she was always hanging out with younger people, so maybe age wasn't as important as it looked. Perhaps she was correct. In fact, because of my age, all of my buddies were older. I didn't connect with kids when I was a kid.

Now I enjoy spending time with the kids and find them intriguing. My three-year-old daughter's remarks to me are so endearing that I can't stand it. I'd much rather speak with her. And I know grownups who are proverbial toddlers and are completely confined in life, as well as folks who are wise for their age.

So awful. Perhaps she is correct. Age is irrelevant. In my previous job, I had always thrown an all-ages party. I want it to be open to everyone. I've never been concerned with attracting a specific demographic; I want everyone to feel welcome. Come on, now. All are welcome. Whether you are one or a hundred. It makes no difference. Actually, it all starts and ends with diapers. If you're fortunate.

For the record, I still don't know how old my mother is. I suppose it must remain a mystery. But age is never an issue with me. It will never be. The person inside the shell is what draws or repels me. When all of my various employers for all of my various activities ask me, "What ages is this for?" "Everyone, hopefully," I always say, because I want an all-ages party. It's a lot more enjoyable!

This year, for my fortieth birthday, I hosted a dinner for all of my lifelong friends. Some were school buddies, mentors, in-laws, and it was certainly a diverse bag of ages, but all of these people mean so much to me. But one of the most fascinating features of the night was that I actually felt my age for the first time in my life. I never got to be a kid when I was younger. Then, in my teens and twenties, I was aggressively attempting to regain my childhood and finally be carefree the way I imagined children could be because I had missed out on that chapter.

I finally feel like a woman. A mom. I have a cheese platter! The fact is that I still feel like a kid at times, but I also believe that I have genuinely intersected with my number. I am forty years old. I am overjoyed. And I am fortunate to say that it feels fantastic!

The contents of this book may not be copied, reproduced or transmitted without the express written permission of the author or publisher. Under no circumstances will the publisher or author be responsible or liable for any damages, compensation or monetary loss arising from the information contained in this book, whether directly or indirectly. .

Disclaimer Notice:

Although the author and publisher have made every effort to ensure the accuracy and completeness of the content, they do not, however, make any representations or warranties as to the accuracy, completeness, or reliability of the content. , suitability or availability of the information, products, services or related graphics contained in the book for any purpose. Readers are solely responsible for their use of the information contained in this book

Every effort has been made to make this book possible. If any omission or error has occurred unintentionally, the author and publisher will be happy to acknowledge it in upcoming versions.

Printed in Great Britain
by Amazon

29824633R00075